Chicano Intermarriage:

A Theoretical and Empirical Study

Chicano Intermarriage:

A Theoretical and
Empirical Study

EDWARD MURGUÍA

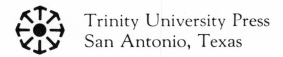

Trinity University Press
San Antonio, Texas

*This work is dedicated
to the memory of my father
DAVID MURGUÍA, SR.,
from Lagos de Moreno, Jalisco, Mexico*

Preface

It is difficult to overstate the importance of inter-ethnic and/or interracial marriage to the study of racial and ethnic relations. Ethnicity is an ascribed criterion; membership in an ethnic or racial group is by birth. Thus, an individual's objective and, to a large part, subjective ethnicity, as well as the ethnicity of his offspring, depends on who his parents were and whom he marries.

The purpose of this book is to examine the condition of the Mexican American people using inter-ethnic marriage, a relatively objective, well-recognized indicator of the extent of ethnic boundary maintenance and social distance.

In the course of this study, it became clear that a statistical analysis of the non-Spanish surname population, comparable to the analysis of the Spanish surnames, could be conducted. It also became apparent that the reason for intermarriage on the part of Anglo Americans could not be subsumed under the assimilation paradigm, which concerns itself with change on the part of the minority in the direction of the majority. Thus, a new theory, "the breaking of ties," is presented in Part Two as an attempt to include both the majority and the minority within a single theoretical framework. In accordance with the theory, parallel statistics are developed for majority as well as minority individuals in this part.

A brief word on terminology. In the Southwest, possession of a Spanish surname is highly correlated with being Mexican American. (The use of Spanish surnames as indicators of Mexican American ethnicity will be examined in more detail in Chapter 7.) Also, in this study the terms "Chicano" and "Mexican American" are used interchangeably to refer to the people in the United States who trace their ancestry to Mexico. It is recognized that the term "Chicano" has connotations of youth and militancy not found in the term "Mexican American"; the current widespread use of "Chicano" to refer to the entire population, however, allows for the interchangeability. The term "Anglo American," or, simply, "Anglo," refers to all non-Spanish surnamed peoples in the United States. Primarily, it refers to the non-Mexican origin white population in the United States.

Work on this project began when I was pursuing graduate studies at the University of New Mexico and, subsequently, at the University of Texas at Austin. Work continued while I was on the faculty at San Francisco State University and, later, at Washington State University. I would like to thank the following for their assistance and encouragement: David Alvírez, then at the University of New Mexico and currently at Pan American University; at the University of Texas at Austin, Professors Harley L. Browning, Walter I. Firey, Armando Gutiérrez (now at the University of Houston), Louis A. Zurcher, and Antonio Ugalde. Professor Browning was particularly generous in providing me with the resources of the Population Research Center at the University of Texas; at San Francisco State University, Professors John W. Kinch, Marjorie J. Seashore, Fred Thalheimer, and Elizabeth Rooney; at Washington State University, the "Gang of Six," my cohort of junior professors at Washington State, namely, Joseph R. DeMartini, William R. Freudenburg, J. Scott Long, Eugene A. Rosa, and Peggy A. Thoits (now at Princeton University), and senior professors Irving Tallman, Marilyn Ihinger-Tallman, Gary R. Lee, Viktor Gecas, William R. Catton, and Riley E. Dunlap.

Richard Ortiz Wilson aided in the coding of the data, and most able secretarial assistance was provided by María Concepción Murguía, Elizabeth A. Leone and Dorothy Howell. Lois Boyd of Trinity University Press, assisted by Virginia Cabello, most competently provided editorial assistance in the final stages of work on the manuscript.

Finally, I am particularly indebted to Professors W. Parker Frisbie and Joe R. Feagin at the University of Texas at Austin, and to my wife, María Concepción Murguía, for their constant support.

Contents

List of Tables and Figures

Table   Page

Table *Page*

Table *Page*

Figure *Page*

Chicano Intermarriage:

A Theoretical and Empirical Study

1 Introduction

The assimilation or non-assimilation of minority groups in the United States has long been of sociological concern. Social scientists have commonly considered the United States as an immigrant society in which peoples of diverse cultural heritage acquire characteristics collectively labeled "American," the process of acquisition of new characteristics and the leaving behind of old traits being called "assimilation."

There is considerable agreement among social scientists that marriage across ethnic lines indicates a weakening of the cohesion of an ethnic group. Ultimately, were intermarriage to occur on a very large scale, the dissolution of the ethnicity as a distinct social entity would result. Milton M. Gordon in *Assimilation in American Life* states, "If marital assimilation . . . takes place fully, the minority group loses its ethnic identity in the larger host or core society."[1] And Mittelbach, et al., say, "Quite generally the marriage patterns of any American ethnic group are a reliable guide to the speed with which such a group is fading into the larger American society."[2]

This study of Mexican American intermarriage will be undertaken from the perspective that intermarriage is the single most conclusive indicator of the amount of assimilation that a minority group has undergone. With this in mind, let us examine the concept of assimilation as it has been developed in the social scientific study of racial and ethnic relations.

The Concept of Assimilation

One of the most firmly established concepts in the sociological study of racial and ethnic relations has been that of assimilation. Simons, writing at the turn of the century, traced the source of the importance of the term back to Ludwig Gumplowicz, "who makes assimilation the most important social fact and considers it the cause of all advance in civilization. To him, the struggle of races was the supreme law of social life, and the resulting 'cross-fertilization of culture,' the cause of progress."[3]

Novicow, a Russian sociologist writing in the nineteenth century, predicted that vast libraries would be written on the concept of assimilation,[4] while Simons herself credited conquest and subsequent assimilation and amalgamation with the rise of civilization. Isolation of peoples and cultures, she believed, led to stagnation and decline.[5]

Park and Burgess make clear the importance and influence the term has had in the United States. The very existence of the nation state, they believed, hinged on the behavior of immigrants as they entered the country throughout its history.[6] They underline the close tie between assimilation and immigration in this manner: "The concept of assimilation, so far as it has been defined in popular usage, gets its meaning from its relation to the problem of immigration."[7]

Robert E. Park contributed to the development of the concept both by an influential definition of the term in the *Encyclopedia of the Social Sciences*[8] and by making it the end process in his well known "race relations cycle."[9]

Milton M. Gordon distinguishes seven stages of assimilation.[10] I have argued elsewhere that the first three stages, cultural assimilation, structural assimilation and marital assimilation are of particular importance,[11] and this study will be concerned primarily with them.

Cultural assimilation, according to Gordon, refers to the adoption by a minority of the attitudinal and behavioral cultural traits of the host society. Structural assimilation, to Gordon, is the formation of primary type relationships between the host and minority groups. Marital assimilation is defined as large-scale intermarriage between the majority and the minority.

In Gordon's view, all minorities in America undergo a fairly rapid cultural assimilation, and if there are no racial and religious barriers[12] between the majority and the minority, the minority will proceed to engage in a process

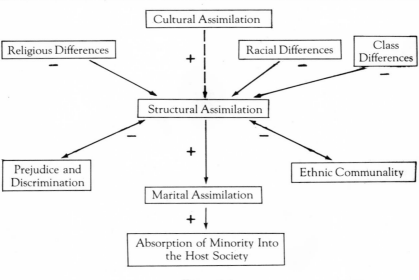

Figure 1.1
The Process of Assimilation

Source: Derived in part from concepts found in Milton M. Gordon, *Assimilation in American Life,* 1964. The broken line between cultural and structural assimilation indicates that cultural assimilation leads to structural assimilation to the extent that racial, religious, and class differences do not interfere.

Table 1.1
Definitions and Relationships of Variables
in the Process of Assimilation

Definitions
1. Cultural assimilation—adopting the norms, rules, values, modes of dress, and language of the majority society.
2. Structural assimilation—widespread primary contacts of a minority group with the majority society.
3. Marital assimilation—large-scale intermarriage between a minority group and the majority society.

Relationships of Variables
The greater the cultural assimilation of the minority, the greater its structural assimilation.
The greater the religious divergence of the minority from the majority, the less its structural assimilation.
The greater the racial divergence of the minority from the majority, the less its structural assimilation.
The greater the class divergence of the minority from the majority, the less its structural assimilation.
The greater the structural assimilation of the minority, the greater its marital assimilation.
The greater the structural assimilation of the minority, the less prejudice and discrimination it experiences.
The greater the prejudice and discrimination directed toward the minority, the less its structural assimilation.
The greater the structural assimilation of the minority, the less ethnic communality it experiences.
The greater the ethnic communality of the minority, the less its structural assimilation.
The greater the marital assimilation of the minority, the greater its absorption into the host society.

---

of structural and marital assimilation.[13] It is clear that were a minority to engage in a large-scale structural and marital assimilation, in time the minority would cease to exist as a distinct entity, since the end product of a process of marital assimilation is amalgamation and complete assimilation. A more detailed set of causal statements involving cultural, structural, and marital assimilation, developed along lines suggested by Blalock,[14] are presented in Table 1 and causally diagrammed in Figure 1. The primary relationships of interest are linked in this model.

At this point, then, let us define the concept of assimilation, keeping in mind the stress on the cultural, structural, and marital stages of assimilation. Assimilation is defined as the process, or the end point of the process, by which two culturally, socially, and genetically distinct populations move toward cultural, social, and genetic homogeneity.[15] Homogeneity does not imply that both populations contribute equally to the end state and, commonly in the United States, minority populations, minor both in size and power, have moved to acquire characteristics of the majority.

The importance of a study of assimilation lies in the bottom line of both Figure 1 and Table 1, namely, in the absorption of a minority into the host society and its eventual disappearance as a distinguishable entity, clearly a momentous occurrence. The interest in the concept of assimilation lies in the complexity of the process of cultural and structural movement toward homogeneity. Also of interest is the fact that some groups in the United States have proceeded much more rapidly than others towards homogeneity. Factors contributing either to homogeneity or to racial and ethnic distinctiveness are of great importance.

Intermarriage as an Indicator of Assimilation

The general concept of assimilation clearly is in need of reliable indicators that will enable an observer to measure the extent of a generally conceived process toward homogeneity. Various indicators, relating to the several subprocesses of assimilation, have been identified and employed to measure the extent of a group's assimilation. Elements of culture in which there is minority-majority divergence, such as in language, music, dress, food, and religious observances, have been used in an attempt to measure the extent of a minority's distinctiveness from a majority.[16] A structural indicator, the extent to which a minority develops primary type relationships with the majority,[17] has also been employed.

Probably the most widely recognized single indicator of the extent of minority assimilation, however, has been intermarriage.[18] Clearly, once large-scale intermarriage between two populations occurs, cultural and social differences have been largely bridged, and genetic differences between the two cannot long remain. On the other hand, a low rate of intermarriage indicates ethnic cohesion and ethnic cultural maintenance.

The Value of a Study of Chicano Intermarriage

There is no doubt in my mind that the general study of intergroup relations is of critical importance. At one extreme one need only look at recent occurrences in Zimbabwe (Rhodesia), the Union of South Africa, or Northern Ireland to realize the conflictual forms such relationships can take within a nation-state. A study such as the one outlined here goes to the core of the subdiscipline of intergroup relations. An examination of the phenomenon of endogamy/exogamy explores the extent to which distinct groups eventually fuse or remain separate, and the conditions under which either phenomenon occurs.

In the United States, too often in the literature of race and ethnic relations has the minority been the single focus of study. Rarely has the majority population been submitted to similar scrutiny, as will be attempted in this project. Characteristics of the non-Spanish surname population will be analyzed in a manner parallel to those of Spanish surname in the empirical sections of this work.[19]

Literature concerned with majority-minority interpersonal contact most often has dealt with racial and religious groups other than the Mexican Americans. It is necessary to put the Chicano experience in perspective, both by using insights gained by researchers studying other groups and by developing new theoretical schemata which will help to explain unique aspects of the Mexican American experience.

Portions of this study will necessarily go beyond the scope of our empirical data; it is hoped that a review of work done by others will provide the materials sufficient at least to generate some hypotheses about Mexican American-Anglo American interpersonal contact, hypotheses which will inform future research.

This study, then, will combine empirical research and statistical analysis, theoretical knowledge gained from previous studies and, hopefully, some personal insight in order to extend our understanding of the dynamic of the Anglo American-Mexican American interpersonal relationship.

Summary

This chapter has concerned itself primarily with the concept of assimilation. We have presented both an analysis and a definition of the concept. We have also pointed out some reasons for the concept's central importance in the area of race and ethnic relations.

Marital assimilation, or intermarriage, determined to be a highly regarded indicator of assimilation, is the indicator to be used in this study. Finally, some reasons for the importance of a study of Anglo American-Mexican American intermarriage, including its basic importance to the subdiscipline of intergroup relations, were given.

Notes

1. Milton M. Gordon, *Assimilation in American Life: The Role of Race, Religion, and National Origins* (New York: Oxford University Press, 1964), p. 80.
2. Frank G. Mittelbach, Joan W. Moore and Ronald McDaniel, *Intermarriage of Mexican-Americans*, Advance Report 6, Mexican American Study Project (Los Angeles: University of California Graduate School of Business Administration, 1966), p. 1.
3. Sarah E. Simons, "Social Assimilation," *American Journal of Sociology*, 6 (May 1901), p. 790.
4. Ibid.
5. Ibid., p. 793.
6. Robert E. Park and Ernest W. Burgess, *Introduction to the Science of Sociology*, 2d ed. (Chicago: The University of Chicago Press, 1924), p. 734.
7. Ibid.
8. Robert E. Park, "Social Assimilation," *Encyclopedia of the Social Sciences*, ed. Alvin Johnson, Vol. II (New York: Macmillan, 1935), pp. 281-2.
9. Robert E. Park, *Race and Culture* (Glencoe, Ill.: The Free Press, 1950), pp. 150ff.
10. Gordon, *Assimilation in American Life*, p. 71. The seven stages or types of assimilation are: cultural, structural, marital, identificational, attitude receptional, behavior receptional and civic.
11. Edward Murguía, *Assimilation, Colonialism and the Mexican American People* (Austin: The Center for Mexican American Studies, The University of Texas at Austin, 1975).
12. Of the two, religious barriers seem to be weaker than racial barriers in the United States. Relative strength of barriers will be examined in detail in Chapter 4. Interestingly Gordon does not use social class as a barrier; its insertion into Table 1 and Figure 1 is a consequence of my own analysis.
13. Gordon, *Assimilation in American Life*, pp. 77-81.
14. Hubert M. Blalock, Jr., *Theory Construction* (Englewood Cliffs, N.J.: Prentice-Hall, 1969).
15. The term can be distinguished from a closely allied concept, acculturation, in that acculturation includes only a process or end point of *cultural* change. Acculturation is but one element of assimilation. Assimilation can also be distinguished from the concept of amalgamation in that amalgamation considers only a process or end point of *genetic* change toward homogeneity.
16. Leo Grebler, Joan W. Moore, and Ralph C. Guzman, *The Mexican American People: The Nation's Second Largest Minority* (New York: The Free Press, 1970), pp. 381-8, 428-32.
17. Ibid., pp. 394-8.
18. Robert K. Merton, "Intermarriage and the Social Structure: Fact and Theory," *Psychiatry*, 4 (August 1941), pp. 363-4; Mittelbach, et al., p. 1.
19. In the Southwest, possession of a Spanish surname is highly correlated with being Mexican American. The use of Spanish surnames as indicators of Mexican American ethnicity will be examined in more detail in Chapter 7.

PART I

A Theoretical and Sociohistorical Study of Chicano Intermarriage

2 Intermarriage and Assimilation

Intermarriage as an Indicator of Assimilation

This chapter will examine the relationship between the concept of assimilation and the variable proposed to be used as its indicator, namely, intermarriage. There are many precedents for the use of intermarriage as an indicator of assimilation, and many researchers have considered it among the most useful. According to Grebler, et al.:

> For most ethnic groups in the United States and elsewhere, the incidence of exogamous marriages has been a reliable guide to the extent and speed of assimilation—their blending with the larger society. Conversely, endogamy can be viewed as a reflection of the rigidity of boundaries around the subpopulation, regardless of whether the boundaries are drawn by majority prejudice against ethnics or by the social and cultural cohesion of the subgroup itself.[1]

William C. Smith claims:

> Intermarriage may be considered the most rigid test of assimilation. When the descendants of immigrants may marry into the dominant group without opposition, it may be assumed that they are accepted and are permitted to participate freely in the life of the older population. So long as relations are restricted solely to economic activities, there is little or no intermarriage. It is only as social contacts of a more intimate nature are permitted that lines are crossed in seeking mates.[2]

Johnson, who compiled data on intermarriage in Bernalillo County, New Mexico, in the late 1940s states: "The amount of intermarriage into the dominant culture group and particularly the trends in the amount, is a good single index of degree and trends in assimilation."[3] And Mittelbach, et al., believe that "Quite generally the marriage patterns of any American ethnic group are a reliable guide to the speed with which such a group is fading into the larger American society."[4]

Taking an opposite point of view, however, Andrew M. Greeley questions the extent to which large-scale intermarriage results in the total assimilation of the minority. He says:

> Those who are interested in studying American ethnic groups often say that the ethnic groups vanish after intermarriage, but there is no evidence to support such an assertion. The child of a Polish mother and an Italian father may choose to define himself as Polish or Italian or Italian-Polish or even only as American, but he is not likely to think of himself as Anglo-Saxon. His personality may show traits that

are more frequent in Poles or Italians, but he is not likely to display a constellation of Yankee or Jewish traits.[5]

No one denies that there is some ethnic maintenance after intermarriage. What is being asserted here, however, is that there is clearly a weakening of ethnic cohesion as a result of intermarriage and that intermarriage encourages a movement away from a definite ethnic identity.

Greeley himself admits that intermarriage has some impact on ethnic boundaries, because in his own example the offspring of a Polish mother and an Italian father will no longer consider himself strictly Polish like his mother, nor Italian like his father.[6] We can speculate that in time, were the Italian-Polish individual to marry an Irish-German person, his children would again be subject to more cultural diversity and would be even less likely to consciously identify with any given ethnicity or unconsciously to have a constellation of traits attributable to any one given ethnicity. Intermarriage does seriously affect ethnicity and ethnic cohesion.[7]

It must be emphasized that cultural assimilation can occur without intermarriage; thus even those who are not products of intermarriage can be moving culturally in the direction of the majority society because of the strength and power of that society's media and school system. Intermarriage, though, does *accelerate* a process of movement away from ethnic homogeneity not only because intrafamilial diversity will result in a loss of cultural reinforcement within one's primary relations but also because without an ethnic familial "united front" the temptation will be to move even more rapidly toward the culture of the majority society. The non-ethnic member of the family can explain and justify his or her cultural ways, which will then seem less alien.

One of the ways in which ethnicity is maintained, according to Greeley, is in an unconscious, covert manner during childhood. An individual, for example, would not necessarily have to consider himself an Italian to act Italian and, therefore, really "be" Italian. Were he raised by an Italian mother, she would unconsciously instill in him traits that can be associated with being Italian.

If Greeley is correct, however, then intermarriage would indeed go to the heart of this covert or unconscious ethnic identity. When a member of an ethnic group intermarries, the non-ethnic partner contributes to instilling, to some extent, his or her differing cultural traits to offspring. Importantly, how much "unconscious ethnicity" can remain after a series of intermarriages?[8]

The Importance of Marital Assimilation in American Society

Let us explore some of the ramifications of marital assimilation in American society. Gunnar Myrdal, in discussing the situation between blacks and whites in the United States, observes, "The practically complete absence of intermarriage in all states has the social effect of preventing the most intimate type of acceptance into white society: if Negroes can never get into a white family, they can never be treated as 'one of the family.' "[9]

While the taboos between Mexican American-Anglo American intermarriage have never been as strict as those against black-white intermarriage, they have existed and persist to the present, particularly when ethnic differences are combined with differences in social class.[10] As we shall see, rates for Chicano-Anglo intermarriage historically have been low, although they have shown somewhat of a tendency to increase in recent years.

One can look at the obverse of the Myrdal quotation in studying the result of one black-white intermarriage. The speaker is a black male who married a Jewish female, with at least one of the results of the intermarriage being a better socioeconomic position for the male.

> I decided to be a truck driver if I could land a job because I figured that it was the best-paying of all the jobs that didn't require an education . . . Well, I found plenty of actual prejudice in the union. I have had all kinds of trouble upon trouble. I still wouldn't have gotten anywhere with this job if it hadn't been for a few Jewish men in this town who heard that my wife is Jewish. When they heard about my older son and heard that we wanted to give him a good Jewish education, these men really opened up a job for me and the union wasn't able to stop me. Negroes just don't find jobs through this union.[11]

Given the American political and economic system, a major means of a minority's attaining full social acceptance in a society hinges upon intermarriage. Suspicion and prejudice develop toward those who remain to themselves. It must be made clear, however, that most often it is not the minority who chooses to remain by itself. The root cause of separatism is the rejection of the minority by the majority. Separatism on the part of a minority group is a reaction to previous prejudice.

There are no biological barriers against intermarriage. The strictures against it are cultural, social, and psychological, and, as mentioned before, commonly it is the majority society, that is, the group in power in the nation-state, that sets the tone of majority-minority relations. This is made clear in the case of the Chicano-Anglo interpersonal dynamic in the following passage, written by a Chicano student at the University of Texas at Austin.

> It seems like only yesterday although I know it was 20 years ago. Twenty years ago in the spring and I was 6. The incident is indelibly etched upon my memory and now I wish to speak of it to make a point

and perhaps cleanse my soul, for in every man there is a small boy crying.

I don't remember her name though Starlight seems to ring true. Surely that could not be it, but I do remember that her name was as beautiful as she; long, golden tresses and big blue eyes, a small, pert nose and a warming smile. I asked if I could carry her books home, and my heart jumped when she said yes. I remember the sun was warm and bright that New Mexican desert day. We spoke in the simple and small words of children, and as I walked her home I knew happiness.

We reached the door of her modest home, and I began my goodbye when her mama came to the door. She reddened with anger when she saw my face and screeched in a voice that rings in my ears still, "What are you doing bringing a Mexican to this house, get inside immediately!" My small friend's bottom was rudely spanked, and the door was slammed in my face. I ran home crying and confused to my mama, relating my tale and beseeching her to tell me what a Mexican was.

That was my first talk with Mama about that and suffice to say not the last. That woman politicized me, but that is another story.[12]

The larger picture of prejudice and discrimination in a nation-state directed against a minority is made up of thousands of similar incidents occurring to minority individuals.

There is a predisposition on the part of the minority, particularly on the part of an upwardly mobile minority, toward interdating and intermarriage. Some would have it that the source of this predisposition is a kind of "brain-washing" by which minorities are convinced that members of their own group are physically unattractive (or, at least, not as attractive as majority individuals) because they depart phenotypically from the Caucasian ideal. The majority society does control the medium of advertising, thus determining what that society will consider ugly or beautiful. An excerpt from a poem by one of the leaders of the Chicano Movement expresses this somewhat. The poem is entitled "22 Miles," the word "miles" representing years of life. The word "gringita" in the poem means an Anglo girl.

looking into blue eyes
wanting to touch a gringita,
ashamed of being Mexican.[13]

The Pros and Cons of Intermarriage

The assimilation of a minority into a majority society can be considered either a positive or a negative occurrence. Undoubtedly, some cultural assimilation, or acculturation, allows members of an ethnicity to come into contact with a wider world. Absorption into the majority's economic structure can provide a higher standard of living. Structural assimilation, that is, the establishment of primary relationships with the majority, breaks down sociocultural barriers, and since usually it has been the majority who has established those barriers, their destruction is a reflection of greater tolerance and of a more open society. On the other hand, if large-scale assimilation occurs, a distinct culture and philosophy with many positive aspects will be lost.

Some assimilation seems to be inevitable when people meet. As Reuter indicates, "There seems to be no historical exception to the rule that when peoples come into contact and occupy the same area there is a mixture of blood."[14] The extent to which intermarriage occurs and the processes by which it is encouraged or discouraged are, of course, what is problematic.[15]

Most often the majority society determines the rate and the extent of contact it will tolerate with a minority, and there are two polar attitudes the majority can take. First, it can be as intolerant and unaccepting as was the United States with blacks during the time of slavery, or as the Union of South Africa is with blacks today. Or it can be relatively open and accepting as the United States has been to white Protestant immigrants coming to its shores. But there is considerable distance between the two ends of that continuum of intolerance and acceptance, and, over time, the extent of acceptance can change. Furthermore, it is clear that if the larger society becomes open to an ethnic or racial group, the solidarity of that group can break down.

Albert I. Gordon points this out with reference to the effect on ethnic minorities of life on college campuses. He says, "Minority groups that advocate the letting down of barriers in fraternities and sororities must accept the responsibility for an increase in intermarriage that follows naturally therefrom."[16] (The groups previously barred from certain fraternities and sororities that Gordon had in mind were Jews, blacks, and Catholics.)

To generalize a bit, advocacy of the breaking down of barriers imposed upon an ethnicity carries with it the responsibility of accelerating the breakdown of the cultural and social solidarity and unity of an ethnic group. This seems to hold true unless mechanisms are found to maintain ethnic cohesion in spite of an absence of prejudice and discrimination.[17]

One possibility for ethnic cohesion is an internal social structure and a territorial arrangement that keeps members of a group from contact with outsiders, as is the case with the Amish and some Native American tribes. But, at this time, such an arrangement does not seem likely to happen with the Mexican American people. An open society results in upward mobility and increased economic advancement, but it also results in the disintegration of ethnic solidarity as measured by increasing rates of intermarriage. This seems to be the price which must be paid for economic advancement and social acceptability in the United States given our present economic system.

There seems little doubt that intermarriage hurries the cultural and structural assimilation of both the ethnic who intermarries and the offspring who result from such a union.[18] What is problematic, we must repeat, is the value approach taken toward intermarriage. On the one hand, some hold that interbreeding (here, genetic, but also, by implication, cultural mixing), is very positive. A biological analogy may be made in which a hybrid plant has qualities superior to those of the two parent stock. On the other hand, some deplore the "mongrelization," the loss of racial and cultural purity, that occurs when there is mixing.

A Positive View of Chicano Intermarriage

Thus, ideologically, one point of view concerning Chicano-Anglo intermarriage is that an increasing rate of intermarriage is a healthy sign, indicating a decrease of prejudice and discrimination and a lowering of barriers dividing peoples in the United States. Just as Chicanos are the result of a Spanish-Indian racial and cultural blending which occurred in the past, so, at present, there is no reason why those historical forces which created the group, that is, the cultural and genetic mixing which created the Mexicano, should be denied them in the present. In intermarriage, ideally, the best of both worlds can be obtained. What, then, makes the prospect of future miscegenation so distasteful?

Those who ideologically oppose intermarriage are often those who understand the deficiencies of American society, and who are sensitive to the prejudice and discrimination endured by the minority and imposed by the majority. They are at the forefront of the attack to obtain wider economic opportunities, a lowering of discriminatory barriers, everything that would increase the standard of living of the minority. Ironically, however, it seems that changes to improve the standard of living of the Chicano minority in the United States will increase the group's probability of assimilation and intermarriage. A liberalism on the part of the majority society, a lessening of prejudice and discrimination, seems to lead to a greater intermingling of ethnic, religious, and racial groups, which in turn leads to higher rates of intermarriage. Clearly, it is difficult not to desire these liberal causal elements, regardless of the consequences for racial and cultural preservation.

One factor in intermarriage, for example, is the college experience, coming at a time in an individual's life when the "risk" of marriage is at its greatest. State-supported institutions of higher learning almost invariably provide individuals contact with members of other groups.[19] Few, however, challenge the fact that a college education is worth the risk.

A Negative View of Chicano Intermarriage

From another perspective, one which comes from viewing events from a colonial, cultural nationalistic perspective, intermarriage is negatively evaluated. Widespread intermarriage, from this point of view, signals the eventual dissolution of a group and a culture; in the case of Chicanos, it represents a capitulation to another group who always has done serious damage to it. It means "selling out" to the majority society, a society which has never really appreciated the Mexican American culture and people.

A particular criticism derives from the fact that sometimes the non-Spanish partner in a mixed marriage is seen as having no real appreciation of the culture and of the people into which he or she is marrying. Not only that, but this person's very presence can change the ambiance of a family gathering. If, for example, he or she speaks no Spanish, then, out of politeness those who naturally speak Spanish in intimate conversations will change to English. And, with an Anglo in the family, it sometimes becomes necessary to move away from doing many of the unique cultural activities commonplace to the ethnicity.[20] Another specific example is that some Anglos have a tendency of mistaking politeness and gentility, a hallmark of the Mexican American culture, for weakness. If an Anglo male marries a Spanish-speaking female, for example, he may exploit her culturally determined gentility, politeness, and sensitivity.

The assumption becomes, then, that although high rates of intermarriage indicate desirable acceptance of a minority group by the majority society, these same high rates indicate a breakdown of ethnic cohesion and solidarity on the part of the minority. If the minority is almost totally in poverty and if the culture of the ethnicity is thought to be a "culture of poverty," maladaptive to twentieth-century modern industrial life, loss of such culture should not be mourned. In the case of the Mexican American people, this view may with some reason be disputed by those who see much of value in the ethnic heritage.

Discrimination and Intermarriage: Attitudes of Anglos Toward Mexicans

Emory Bogardus's well-regarded social distance scale has documented the low esteem in which the people of the United States generally hold Mexicans and Mexican Americans. The Bogardus social distance scale[21] is reproduced in Table 2.1. Of particular interest to us is item one, willingness to marry, the most difficult barrier for the total social acceptance of an ethnic group in the Bogardus scale.

Thirty ethnic groups were included in the Bogardus surveys, a number of which were taken over several decades, and on the basis of the respondents' answers, each ethnicity was given a racial distance quotient. The lowest possible score for an ethnic group on the quotient is a 1.00, which indicates

Table 2.1
The Bogardus Social Distance Scale

I would willingly admit members of _____ ethnic group or race:
1. to close kinship by marriage
2. to my club as personal chums
3. to my street as neighbors
4. to employment in my occupation
5. to citizenship in my country
6. as visitors only to my country
7. would exclude from my country

Source: James W. Vander Zanden, *American Minority Relations*, 2d ed., 1966, pp. 72-3.

total acceptance of the ethnic group by the respondents, even to the point of willingness to intermarry with a member of that group. A score of 7.00 indicates complete rejection, to the point of exclusion from the United States.

The racial distance quotient and rank of Mexican Americans and Mexicans is given in Table 2.2. Mexican Americans and Mexicans have made very slow absolute and no relative progress up the social distance scale in the forty years surveyed here. While there have been some absolute gains, from 2.52 to 2.37 for Mexican Americans, and from 2.69 to 2.56 for Mexicans, both groups have lost ground relative to the other groups. Of the thirty groups in the survey, Mexican Americans dropped from the twenty-first most desirable group to the twenty-third, and Mexicans dropped from twenty-second to twenty-eighth.[22]

Also, Mexicans did not fare well in Albert I. Gordon's survey of students at forty-four American colleges and universities. Gordon, using a social distance scale similar to that developed by Bogardus, states:

> The attitude toward the Mexican is also generally unfriendly. Our all-school sample indicates that less than one-third of all our student sample of 5,407 would marry a Mexican while 45 percent would date or allow a son or daughter to date a Mexican. Fourteen percent of the all-school sample would bar a Mexican from living on the same block while 15 percent would bar him from any social or recreational life in which the average student in our sample is involved. . . .Clearly neither Filipino nor Mexican is *persona grata* to the average American college or university student.[23]

More generally, it is documented that elements of prejudice and discrimination have been with the United States since its founding. In fact, in the Declaration of Independence, Thomas Jefferson has this to say about

Table 2.2
Racial Distance Quotient and Rank for Selected Groups,
the Bogardus Social Distance Scale, 1926-1966

Year	Mexican Americans		Mexicans	
	RDQ	Rank	RDQ	Rank
1926	–	21	2.69	22
1946	2.52	22	2.89	24
1956	2.51	22	2.79	28
1966	2.37	23	2.56	28

Year	Group Ranking Highest			Group Ranking Lowest		
		RDQ	Rank		RDQ	Rank
1926	English	1.06	1	East Indians	3.91	30
1946	American (U.S. white)	1.04	1	Japanese	3.61	30
1956	American (U.S. white)	1.08	1	Koreans	2.80	30
1966	American (U.S. white)	1.07	1	Indians from India	2.62	30

Source: Emory S. Bogardus, "Comparing Racial Distance in Ethiopia, South Africa, and the United States," *Sociology and Social Research*, 52 (January 1968), p. 152.

the Native Americans: "He [King George III] has excited domestic Inhabitants of our Frontiers, the merciless Indian Savages, whose known Rule of Warfare is an undistinguished destruction of all Ages, Sexes, and Conditions."

Summary and Conclusion

In this chapter, the validity of the relationship between assimilation and its indicator, intermarriage, has been examined. Discussed in detail were both the positive and negative consequences of intermarriage, the major positive one being that intermarriage, signaling majority tolerance and acceptance, may result in the minority's more rapid upward mobility, while negatively, intermarriage seriously threatens ethnic cultural maintenance and social cohesion.

Finally, studies by Emory Bogardus and A. I. Gordon demonstrated that, to date, Mexican Americans have not been a highly accepted minority group in American society.

Notes

1. Leo Grebler, Joan W. Moore, and Ralph C. Guzman, *The Mexican American People: The Nation's Second Largest Minority* (New York: The Free Press, 1970), p. 406. Low black, Chicano, and Asian American intermarriage rates have usually been interpreted as resulting from majority prejudice and discrimination, but studies of the upper class and of white ethnics have emphasized in-group solidarity as being causal.

2. William C. Smith, *Americans in the Making: The National History of Assimilation of Immigrants* (New York: D. Appleton-Century Company, Inc., 1939), p. 359. By relations "restricted solely to economic activities," Smith seems to be indicating impersonal relationships usually referred to as secondary relationships. Smith's "social contacts of a more intimate nature" obviously refers to primary relationships. Smith's statement, however, does not indicate the process by which a minority moves from secondary to primary relationships with the majority.

3. Cited in Nancie L. González, *The Spanish-Americans of New Mexico: A Heritage of Pride* (Albuquerque: University of New Mexico Press, 1969), p. 165.

4. Frank G. Mittelbach, Joan W. Moore, and Ronald McDaniel, *Intermarriage of Mexican-Americans* (Los Angeles: Graduate School of Business Administration, University of California at Los Angeles, 1966), p. 1. It must be noted, however, that cultural influence between Anglo Americans and Mexican Americans has not been all in a single direction. While it is undeniable that, by and large, because of the size of the majority society, its strength and influence as well as its advanced technology, most cultural change has been minority change in the direction of the majority, it is clear that Mexicans have profoundly influenced the culture and life-style of the majority, in architecture, cuisine, even in pace of life, manners, and language in many areas of the Southwest. One need only observe Anglo Americans in Texas border towns in which they constitute the minority to realize this. This is true as well in the state of New Mexico, where because of Hispanic numerical and historical importance, Chicanos (or Hispanos as some New Mexicans prefer) continue to strongly influence Anglo Americans.

5. Andrew M. Greeley, *Ethnicity in the United States: A Preliminary Reconnaissance* (New York: John Wiley and Sons, 1974), p. 313.

6. The very fact that a Pole and an Italian met and married indicates a weakening of ethnic boundaries.

7. Also, those born of an intermarriage would probably be more likely not to consider ethnic boundaries important (to do so would involve a psychological contradiction because they themselves are not ethnically homogeneous) and so would be more likely to engage in future intermarriages than would the progeny of an ethnically homogenous home.

8. In contrast, in conscious or self-identificational ethnicity, an individual could claim an ethnicity as his own even if he were the product of an intermarriage and regardless of his cultural traits.

9. Gunnar Myrdal, *An American Dilemma: The Negro Problem and Modern Democracy* (New York: Harper and Brothers, 1944), p. 607.

10. That is, if the Mexican is of a lower social class than the Anglo.

11. Albert I. Gordon, *Intermarriage* (Boston: Beacon Press, 1964), p. 280. Of course, we must be careful not to overgeneralize from this example, for what happens to individuals in a mixed marriage depends upon the amount of acceptance they

receive. Were the individuals in this example to have been ostracized, no help would have been forthcoming.

12. Jim Coronado, "Ladies, Allay Men's Fears: Ask a Guy to Lunch Today," *The Daily Texan*, The University of Texas at Austin, Austin, Texas, 5 May 1977.

13. José Angel Gutiérrez, "22 Miles," *Aztlan: An Anthology of Mexican American Literature*, ed. Stan Steiner (New York: Vintage Books, 1972), p. 330.

14. E. B. Reuter, quoted by Brewton Berry in *Race and Ethnic Relations*, 3d ed. (Boston: Houghton Mifflin Company, 1965), pp. 273-74.

15. Note, however, that there may be interbreeding without intermarriage, as occurred with the black slaves in the South.

16. Albert I. Gordon, *Intermarriage*, p. 53.

17. The Jewish population in the United States today seriously feels the threat of lack of cohesion due to lack of outside pressure, that is, ironically, a lack of sufficient prejudice and discrimination necessary to keep the group together.

18. Undeniably, there is some counterinfluence and it needs to be examined in future work.

19. Although not totally. See John F. Scott, "The American College Sorority: Its Role in Class and Ethnic Endogamy," *American Sociological Review*, 30 (August 1965), pp. 514-27. Scott sees sororities as an attempt by parents of college women to maintain endogamy by race and by social class.

20. It must be noted, however, that non-Spanish surnamed individuals who intermarry with Mexicans vary greatly in their attitudes toward the culture. Some are most accepting of the language and customs. Others are intolerant, look at the Mexican culture as inferior and to be forgotten, and want as little as possible to do with other Mexicans and the Mexican culture. These can keep their mates from participation in ethnic events and customs.

21. In James W. Vander Zanden, *American Minority Relations*, 2d ed. (New York: The Ronald Press Company, 1966), pp. 72-3.

22. In 1956, Mexicans ranked lower than Negroes in social distance. In 1966, Mexicans were in a tie with blacks with a racial distance quotient of 2.56. Gunnar Myrdal, in his classic *An American Dilemma*, said of Mexicans, "In many parts of the country, Mexicans are kept in a status similar to the Negro's or only a step above." Gunnar Myrdal, *An American Dilemma* , p. 53.

23. Albert I. Gordon, *Intermarriage*, pp. 26-7.

3 The American Class Structure and Chicano Intermarriage

Given that the strength of ethnic boundaries can be determined by rates of intermarriage, the relationship between Spanish surnames and non-Spanish surnames can be visualized as being similar to Figure 3.1

The line separating the Spanish surname from the non-Spanish surname populations becomes more permeable the higher the social class.

Social distance seems to be greatest between lower class Anglos[1] and poor, barrio-inhabiting Chicanos, who sometimes need not come into contact with Anglos at all when living in large ethnic enclaves and who rarely come into contact with members of the majority society at a primary group level. On their part, the poorer classes of the majority society, because of their own status insecurity, are often among the most prejudiced and discriminatory of the majority society towards minorities.[2]

When primary level contacts between Anglos and Chicanos occur, they seem to occur more frequently within the middle and upper classes, so that, as indicated, the vertical line separating the lower ethclasses[3] is heavier and less permeable than is the line separating the middle and upper ethclasses.

At the elite levels of society, there has been more interpersonal contact between Mexicans and Anglos than at the lower levels. Simmons, in commenting on the social life in certain established Texas/Mexico border communities where Mexican Americans outnumber Anglo Americans, says:

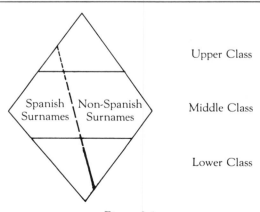

Upper Class

Spanish Surnames | Non-Spanish Surnames

Middle Class

Lower Class

Figure 3.1
Social Class and Chicano Intermarriage

the small Anglo minority jointly participates with Mexican Americans
·. . . and social interaction is ordered on a class basis rather than an
ethnic basis. There exist close friendships between Anglos and Mexicans, home visiting and entertaining, and a much greater amount of
intermarriage. Starr County, like Brownsville and Laredo, has a long
tradition of intermingling between Anglo and Mexican . . .[4]

From the Chicano side of it, Mittelbach, et al. observe: "There are hints
from other studies that rising upper-middle class individuals replace some of
their ethnic culture with a more diffuse culture based on their class status,
and that this process makes intermarriage easier for them."[5] In other words,
as Chicanos attain middle-class status, distinctions based on ethnicity
between them and the Anglo majority diminish and social class more accur-
ately describes their cultural and social life than does ethnicity.

In general, the condition of being middle class in the United States tends
to dilute ethnicity. With middle-class status comes increased participation in
the activities of the majority society; this results in less use of the Spanish
language and less contact with one's extended family. In the middle class,

Table 3.1
Chicano Intermarriage by Occupational Status
of Males, Los Angeles County, 1963

Occupational Status of Males	Percentage of Exogamous Males	Percentage of Exogamous Females
High[a]	40.4	50.7
Middle[b]	22.1	28.1
Low[c]	21.4	19.7
Total[d]	23.6	26.9
Total[d] (Males and Females Combined) 25.3		

[a]High: Professional, technical and kindred workers, managers, officials and proprietors (except farm).

[b]Middle: Clerical, sales and kindred workers, craftsmen, foremen and kindred workers, and farm owners and managers.

[c]Low: Operatives and kindred workers, non-household service workers, private household workers, laborers, and farm workers.

[d]Totals include individuals whose occupations were not reported.

Source: Derived from Mittelbach, et al., *Intermarriage of Mexican-Americans*, Table III-1, p. 21 and Table II-4, p. 15. Note that both males and females were categorized according to the occupational category of the male in the marriage. The female then is given the status *into* *which* she is marrying, while the male is given his *current* occupational status. Although this makes the male and female statistics not comparable, it does not affect our major point that high class standing is associated with outmarriage.

there is an increased amount of contact with the specialized group of people with whom one works and, as one moves up in class standing, these work associates tend less and less to be of Mexican ethnicity. Also, because upward mobility often involves geographical mobility, there is more contact with the non-Spanish surname society, particularly if one moves outside of the Southwest where the numbers of one's fellow ethnics are small.[6]

Mittelbach, et al. state: "Both the implied rejection of the traditional (especially by the young) and the implied acceptance of a social class culture rather than an ethnic culture among middle-class Mexican Americans seem to spell out a growing dynamic of change."[7] What seems to be occurring is a move from a working-class ethnic culture to a middle-class culture, indistinguishable from that of the majority society except for some cultural externals, traces of the old ethnicity in some food, some Spanish phrases, and some household decorations.[8]

Empirical proof for our contention that middle-class status weakens ethnicity is to be found in the Mittelbach, et al. study of intermarriage in Los Angeles.[9] The authors report that intermarriage increases as one rises in occupational status. (See Table 3.1.)

Occupation is considered to be one of the major indicators of social class; thus social class is an important factor in exogamy. It follows that the higher the social class of Chicanos, the more likely they are to intermarry. This class finding is important because Mexican Americans in the Southwest are experiencing a rise, although not a major rise, in relative and absolute economic standing. For example, from 1959 to 1969 in the Southwest, the income for Chicano males, 25 to 64 years of age, rose from 63 to 66 percent of that of Anglo males and the income for Chicano females rose from 67 to 76 percent of that of all whites.[10]

Indirect support for our contention that rates of intermarriage rise with an increase of class standing can be derived from Thomas's study of the effect of social class on Catholic intermarriage,[11] a high percentage of Mexican Americans being Catholic. Thomas found that the rates of outmarriage for Catholics varied directly by social class. In a large metropolitan area, rates of outmarriage were 8.5 percent in the lowest rental areas, 17.9 percent in the highest rental areas, and 19.3 percent in suburban areas of the city.

Lack of class equality was a factor that led to a derogatory attitude toward Mexicans by Anglos in the early days of inter-ethnic contact after the Anglo conquest of the Southwest. McWilliams believes that:

> The absence of local self-government and the presence of a population that was seven-eighths illiterate in 1850, predisposed the Anglo-Americans to form an extremely negative opinion of the Mexican lower classes who constituted nine-tenths of the population. If a larger

middle-class element had existed, the adjustment between the two cultures might have been facilitated and the amount of intermarriage might have been greater.[12]

Here the primary emphasis for the lack of Anglo tolerance toward Mexicans is placed not directly on prejudice and discrimination on the part of the majority individuals, but on a difference in social class. Anglos coming into the territories had a middle-class orientation; Mexicans were largely lower class and therefore exploitable.

More currently, Cesar Chavez sees class factors, as opposed to the attitude and behavior of individuals, as causal for the conflict between Anglos and Mexicans. Specifically, Chavez is referring to Anglo farm owners and Mexican farm workers in the Southwest.

> In the beginning, there was a lot of nonsense about the poor farm worker: "Gee, the farm worker is poor and disadvantaged and on strike, he must be a super human being!" That was my opening speech: "Look, you're here working with a group of men; the farm worker is only a human being. You take the poorest of these guys and give him that ranch over there, he could be just as much of a bastard as the guy sitting there right now. Or if you think that all growers are bastards, you're no good to us either. Remember that both are men."[13]

In other words, the problems between the two groups are class-related and economic in nature. Looking at social class as causal leaves open an eventual acceptance of intermarriage between Chicano and Anglo. Fundamentally, the barrier between the two is economic, rather than racial or ethnic, and therefore some Anglos who are of a similar social class as most Mexicans cease to be oppressors. In fact, some Raza, because of their class position, themselves become oppressors. The above is, in essence, a Marxian analysis which sees class rather than ethnicity as the primary basis for conflict between groups of people.

Although there is truth in the above view, clearly ethnicity cannot be disregarded as an important analytical tool, because historically it provided the basis for much class categorization. Also, ethnic and racial discrimination continue to exist, but particularly when ethnicity and race interact with poverty, producing multiplicative, rather than additive, ill effects.

Class Versus Cultural Definition of an Out-Group

Of importance to this study is the out-group concept of "Anglo" as used by the Chicano minority. In certain contexts, it has extremely negative connotations. In these cases, it refers to members of the majority society as a whole who are seen to contain within themselves all the undesirable aspects attributable to that society—a coldness, a mercenary, exploitative attitude toward others, particularly toward powerless others, a group proud of their fair hair and light skin who sees as inferior all those who are not similar to them. Intermarriage with such a group is scarcely to be desired.

Another interpretation of the concept would have it that what distinguishes people within the United States has more to do with their class standing than with their culture or race. From this point of view, Anglos can be considered in a positive or negative light primarily on the basis of their individual class position in the social structure, rather than on the basis of their biological or cultural characteristics.

In justifying intermarriage, some Raza who are intermarried are sometimes heard to say about their spouse, "Es mas Chicano/a que muchos Chicanos/as," which translates, "He (or she) is more Chicano (Chicana) than many Chicanos (Chicanas)." This means that the Anglo spouse is more sensitive to and partakes of the culture more than many who are born into it. If this comment is not simply a rationalization, then it indicates that personal characteristics can sometimes override the lack of an inherent ethnicity.

Another justification for intermarriage is the observation that if both Chicano and Anglo are solidly middle class, there does not seem to be that much cultural difference between the two. Along these lines, Cesar Chavez has commented on what he sees as a "reverse prejudice."

> I hear *la raza* more and more . . . . Some people don't look at it as racism, but when you say *la raza*, you are saying an anti-gringo thing, and our fear is that it won't stop there. Today it's anti-gringo, tomorrow it will be anti-Negro, and day after it will be anti-Filipino, anti-Puerto Rican. And then it will be anti-poor-Mexican, and anti-darker-skinned-Mexican.[14]

Chavez is consistent in looking at the farmworker problem as being an economic rather than ethnic one, and he is correct in that an overemphasis of the superiority of one's own ethnicity could lead to a denial of the humanity and dignity of others, which could, in the end, turn out to be counterproductive.

Among Chicano academicians, however, there seems to be a current move away from the use of a colonial model of exploitation which emphasizes race and ethnicity as the basis of oppression, toward a Marxist model which emphasizes class-based oppression.[15] In the Marxist model, the oppressors are those of the ruling class; in the colonial model, although a wide divergence in social class between oppressor and oppressed is implied, the major focus is on a difference in race and ethnicity. Two basic reasons seem to be operative in this shift from a colonial model to a Marxist model: first, as Chicanos move into the middle class, the concern by Chicano academicians for the oppressed lower classes cannot rely solely on ethnicity; secondly, radical movements are often supported by Anglos (this is particularly visible at universities). These Anglos often can be even more radical than ethnics, but in a colonial ideology, Anglos automatically fall into the category of oppressor. This dissonance often leads to a modification of theories of oppression.

The change from a colonial model to a class model of oppression has important implications for a study of Chicano intermarriage because a paradigm based on ethnicity and the maintenance of a cultural heritage will not favor ethnic intermarriage. On the other hand, a paradigm based on the removal of the inequalities of class will not overly concern itself with ethnic intermarriage. Ultimately, however, and by definition, an ethnic analysis of a situation cannot totally become a class analysis. Thus, for those who define themselves as students of the Mexican American population, ethnicity will have to be maintained as an organizing category at least to some extent.

Summary and Conclusion

In this chapter, we have looked at American class structure and its relationship to Chicano exogamy. Importantly, it was indicated that: first, high class status exposes Mexican Americans to greater interpersonal and cultural contact with the majority society; second, there is a direct relationship between social class and Chicano intermarriage; and third, Chicanos as a whole are experiencing a slow rise in social standing in the United States. It follows, then, that as the Chicano population slowly moves toward middle-class status, the rate of Chicano intermarriage should be expected to increase slowly.

In an ethnic analysis, the outgroup (in this case, Anglo Americans), defined primarily by racial and cultural criteria, is seen as exploitative; in a class analysis groups are considered exploitative on the basis of their position in a social structure. It was indicated that there has been an increased emphasis in class analysis by Chicano social scientists. However, this shift from an ethnic analysis to a class analysis by social scientists who use ethnicity as the basis of their studies will be, of necessity, less than total.

Notes

1. Characteristics of majority individuals associated with prejudice and discrimination consciously or unconsciously by Chicanos include a southern rural accent, western attire, and poverty. Of course, in reality the correlation between these characteristics and prejudice and discrimination is not perfect.
2. A good summary of structural factors in prejudice and discrimination can be found in Chapter 4 of James W. Vander Zanden's *American Minority Relations* (New York: The Ronald Press Company, 1966), pp. 101-35.

3. Ethclass is a term developed by Milton M. Gordon and refers to the combination of ethnicity and social class of a subgroup. He defines it as "the subsociety created by the intersection of the vertical stratifications of ethnicity with the horizontal stratifications of social class." "Lower-class Chicanos" or "middle-class Italians" would be two examples of ethclass. Milton M. Gordon, *Assimilation in American Life* (New York: Oxford University Press, 1964), p. 51.

4. John S. Shockley, *Chicano Revolt in a Texas Town* (Notre Dame, Ind.: University of Notre Dame Press, 1974), p. 254n.

5. Frank G. Mittelbach, Joan W. Moore and Ronald McDaniel, *Intermarriage of Mexican Americans* (Los Angeles: Graduate School of Business Administration, University of California at Los Angeles).

6. The Mexican American people have traditionally resided in the five Southwestern states of Texas, New Mexico, Colorado, Arizona, and California; however, significant Chicano populations reside in the Midwest and in the remaining Western states.

   Mittelbach, et al. believe that social mobility, both horizontal and vertical, weakens ethnic ties. They say: "It is well known that both changing residence and moving up or down in the social structure tend to weaken the ties between an individual and his ethnic group." Mittelbach, et al., *Intermarriage of Mexican Americans*, p. 3. However, this researcher hypothesizes that for Mexican Americans, downward mobility may cause a return to the subculture of the barrio, which would strengthen rather than weaken ties. And clearly, a geographical move from a region such as the Northeast with relatively few fellow ethnics to one with many, such as in the Southwest, cannot help but increase ethnic contact.

7. Ibid., p. 46.

8. Countervailing forces are the large size of the Chicano population in many areas which makes for cultural reinforcement, continuous emigration from Mexico, and the close proximity of the border.

9. Mittelbach, et al., *Intermarriage of Mexican Americans*, pp. 19-26.

10. Vernon M. Briggs, Walter Fogel, and Fred Schmidt, *The Chicano Worker* (Austin: The University of Texas Press, 1977), p. 61. Here, the difference between the male and female calculations is that Chicano males are compared with non-Chicano males while Chicano females are compared with all whites of which they are a part. The two calculations are roughly comparable, however.

11. John L. Thomas, "The Factor of Religion in the Selection of Marriage Mates," *American Sociological Review*, 16 (August 1951), pp. 487-91.

12. Carey McWilliams, *North From Mexico* (New York: Greenwood Press, 1968), p. 75.

13. Peter Matthiessen, *Sal Si Puedes: Cesar Chavez and the New American Revolution* (New York: Dell Publishing Company, 1973), p. 105.

14. Ibid., p. 130.

15. The relationship between academics studying and involved in a popular movement and the people in the movement is a complex one. Often, academics leap ahead of a popular movement by following lines of thought and action to their logical conclusions. But often events outside of academia moving in directions contrary to expectations force some scholars to reevaluate their theories and the assumptions upon which they rest.

4 *Barriers to Intermarriage*

Types of Intermarriage

Most students of factors in mate selection first postulate a basic homogeneity between two individuals who select each other and then try to explain deviations from homogeneity. Thus, similarities in race, religion, social class, and ethnicity are hypothesized and usually found.[1]

When one thinks of an intermarriage, a marriage across some social boundary or barrier, the intermarriage is usually one of four types: 1) an interracial marriage, 2) an interfaith marriage,[2] 3) an interclass marriage, or 4) an interethnic marriage.

A Chicano-Anglo intermarriage generally is not considered an interracial marriage because, for the most part, Chicanos have been classified as Caucasians. Nevertheless, Chicanos are a combination of Caucasian European and Native American stock, and those who emphasize the Native American ancestry of Chicanos consequently consider Chicano-Anglo marriages as interracial.

Chicano-Anglo intermarriages may or may not be interfaith marriages depending on the religion of the two individuals marrying. Since most non-Spanish surname persons in the United States are Protestant while most Spanish surname individuals are Catholic, many Chicano-Anglo unions are interfaith marriages.

Mexican Americans have been more highly concentrated in the lower socioeconomic levels of American society than have Anglo-Americans. As a result, Chicano-Anglo intermarriages not infrequently have been interclass marriages. A Chicano-Anglo intermarriage is, above all, an interethnic marriage, a marriage of individuals of differing national origins.

Relative Strengths of the Four Barriers

According to Udry, "the more significant to a society are the differences between two categories of people, the less will they intermarry,"[3] and several studies have been done from which we can partially measure the relative strength of the four variables of race, ethnicity, religion, and class. Albert I. Gordon asked college students to estimate the difficulty of different types of intermarriages. The five possible responses were: 1) hardest, 2) next hardest, 3) not quite so hard, 4) fairly easy, and 5) easiest. In Table 4.1, the first column indicates the percentage of individuals who replied either "hardest" or "next hardest" to a given type of exogamy. The second column indicates percentages of those who replied "easiest" and "fairly easy" to the type of intermarriage.

Table 4.1
Types of Exogamy by Order of Difficulty

Type	High Difficulty (%)	Low Difficulty (%)
1. Racial Exogamy	91	6
2. Religious Exogamy	50	27
3. Educational Exogamy		
(Future Social Class)	31	39
4. Ethnic Exogamy	16	58
5. Economic Class Exogamy		
(Past Social Class)	13	54

Source: Adapted from Albert I. Gordon, *Intermarriage*, pp. 36-7.

Educational exogamy (intermarriage with someone of a different education) can be considered an indicator of social class exogamy, just as education (along with income and occupation) is usually considered an indicator of social class. For these college student respondents, educational exogamy probably indicates the *future* social class of an individual while economic class exogamy indicates *past* social class, i.e., the social class of an individual's parents.

Therefore, there are indications that in the United States, racial barriers to intermarriage are strongest, followed distantly by religious barriers. Disparity in future social class is the next important barrier in intermarriage, followed by ethnicity, and, finally, past social class.

Additional evidence for my estimation of the relative strengths of variables in intermarriage is derived from a study by Strauss (Table 4.2). If assumptions similar to those made regarding Table 4.1 are in effect, namely, that educational status indicates future class status and that social background indicates past class status, or more properly, the status of the individual's parents, the relative strengths of the variables are the same as in the Gordon study. (Unfortunately, Strauss does not have a satisfactory indicator of ethnicity.)[4]

The variables of race, religion, and ethnicity can be examined in more detail, using a categorization devised by W. Lloyd Warner and Leo Srole (Table 4.3). Warner and Srole developed a schema by which cultural, racial, and religious types are placed in order of their assimilative potential. The "host society" or the group in the United States into which all other racial and ethnic groups assimilate is understood to be white (light Caucasoid), Anglo Saxon (English-speaking), and Protestant.

The twin bases of their typology are race (one of our variables of interest) and culture. Culture, to Warner and Srole, is composed of two elements, religion (a second variable of interest) and language. Language in the Warner and Srole typology closely approximates ethnicity, our third variable of interest. Thus, three of the four variables of most interest in this analysis of intermarriage, namely, race, religion, and ethnicity, form the basis of their categorization.

Empirical validation of the Warner and Srole typology comes from Wessel's study of Woonsocket, Rhode Island. Wessel examined intermarriage rates for ethnic groups in the area and found that the highest rates of outmarriage were among the British, followed by the Irish, French-Canadians, Slavs, Italians, and Jews, in that order.[5] Using the Warner and

Table 4.2

Percent Exclusion of Individuals as Marriage Partners

Variables	Males Who Would Exclude (%)	Females Who Would Exclude (%)
Race	49.7	65.5
Religion	41.6	42.5
Educational Status (Future Social Class)	33.5	40.5
Social Background (Past Social Class)	27.8	34.0

Source: Anselm Strauss, cited in Udry, *The Social Context of Marriage*, p. 205.

Table 4.3

Cultural and Racial Types in Order of
Their Assimilative Potential

Cultural Types	Racial Types
I. English-speaking Protestants	I. Light Caucasoids
II. Protestants who do not speak English	II. Dark Caucasoids
III. English-speaking Catholics and other non-Protestants	III. Mongoloid and Caucasoid mixtures with a Mediteranean appearance
IV. Catholics and other non-Protestants most of whom speak allied Indo-European languages	IV. Mongoloids and mixed peoples with a predominantly Mongoloid appearance
V. English-speaking non-Christians	V. Negroes and all Negroid mixtures
VI. Non-Christians who do not speak English	

Source: W. Lloyd Warner and Leo Srole, *Social Systems of American Ethnic Groups*, pp. 286-8.

Srole schema, one sees that *racially* the British, Irish, French-Canadians, and Slavs are Type I, while the Italians and Jews are Type II. *Culturally*, the British are Type I, the Irish are Type III, the French-Canadian, Slavs, and Italians are Type IV, and the Jews are Type VI. The order, then, in which Wessel's ethnic groups outmarry both by race and by culture is the same as the order of Warner and Srole's cultural and racial types.[6]

Approximately thirty years after the Wessel study, Albert I. Gordon studied attitudes toward intermarriage held by university students throughout the United States. In reply to a question as to whether the students would marry a person of a given ethnicity, race, or religion, Gordon reports the following responses, as presented in Table 4.4.

Table 4.4
Respondents Replying in The Affirmative to
the Question, "I would marry a ＿＿＿＿＿＿＿＿＿＿."

	I		II		III	
	Catholic Ethnics		Non-Caucasians		Religions	
Light or Dark Caucasians	Italians	65%	Negroes	29%	Protestant	74%
	Irish	64%	Japanese	24%	Catholic	56%
	Polish	61%			Jews	37%
Mixed Caucasians	Mexicans	31%				

Source: Derived from Albert I. Gordon, *Intermarriage*, pp. 18-32.

Notice that the three subtables in Table 4.4 largely follow the Warner and Srole typology. When religion is held constant as in the first subtable where all of the groups are Catholic, both the light and dark Caucasians are clearly more acceptable than the mixed Caucasian Mexicans.[7]

The Four Major Barriers to Chicano-Anglo Intermarriage

Historically, then, there have been four barriers to large-scale Chicano-Anglo intermarriage, namely, the differences between the two groups in race, religion, class, and ethnicity. When the generalized differences between the two groups developed in Table 4.5 do not apply, either because of change over time or because the generalizations do not adequately describe individuals in either of the two populations, the probability of intermarriage increases.

Table 4.5

The Four Major Barriers to Chicano-Anglo Intermarriage

Intermarriage Categories	Mexican Americans	Anglo Americans
1. Race	Mixed Caucasian (Nat. Am. + Cauc.)	Light Caucasian
2. Religion	Catholic	Protestant
3. Social class	Lower class	Middle and upper class
4. Ethnicity or national origin	Spanish language and customs	English language and customs

Thus, over time, a considerable amount of cultural assimilation among many of the Mexican minority has taken place, so that divergence by ethnicity has been minimized. With reference to social class, a significant number of Chicanos have moved into the lower middle and middle classes, particularly since the Second World War. Some Mexican Americans are Protestant, and some are phenotypically indistinguishable from the majority society, displaying clearly Caucasian physical characteristics.

Looking at it from the side of the majority society, those Anglo Americans who are lower middle[8] and middle class and those who are Catholic are the most likely candidates for intermarriage with Chicanos. Precisely where there is convergence within the four categories is intermarriage more likely to take place.

Summary and Conclusion

It was determined in this chapter that there are four major barriers to intermarriage in the United States. These barriers consist of divergences in the four most important ways that people group or categorize themselves in America, namely, by race, religion, social class, and ethnicity.

By examining various studies, the relative strength of the four barriers was determined. The strongest barrier was race, followed by religion, social class, and ethnicity, in that order. Upon examining social class in more detail, it appeared that future social class, or the perceived class of an individual as an adult, was stronger than ethnicity, but that past social class, or the class of an individual's parents, was weaker than ethnicity.

To some extent, Chicanos vary from the majority society along each of the four dimensions. Where there is convergence, the greatest amount of intermarriage is likely to take place.

Notes

1. The literature on homogamy is extensive. A general study is Ernest W. Burgess and Paul Wallin, "Homogamy in Social Characteristics," *American Journal of Sociology*, 49 (September 1943), pp. 109-24. For homogamy by social class see Richard Centers, "Marital Selection and Occupational Strata," *American Journal of Sociology*, 54 (May 1949), pp. 530-35, and August B. Hollingshead, "Cultural Factors in the Selection of Marriage Mates," *American Sociological Review*, 15 (October 1950), pp. 619-27. For homogamy by religion, see John L. Thomas, "The Factor of Religion in the Selection of Marriage Mates," *American Sociological Review*, 16 (August 1951), pp. 487-91; and Paul C. Glick, "Intermarriage and Fertility Patterns Among Persons in Major Religious Groups," *Eugenics Quarterly*, 7 (1960), pp. 31-8. For homogamy by education, see Paul C. Glick, *American Families* (New York: John Wiley and Sons, Inc., 1958), p. 117.

2. A religious intermarriage is often called a "mixed marriage." By common usage, a mixed marriage ceases to be so if one of the partners converts to the other's faith. Thus, a religious intermarriage can begin as an intermarriage and later cease to be so, unlike interracial and interethnic marriages. Religious intermarriages share this characteristic with social class outmarriages.

3. J. Richard Udry, *The Social Context of Marriage* (Philadelphia: J. B. Lippencott Company, 1966), p. 204.

4. Since the questions asked of the respondents were not the same, the actual percentages of those responding to each variable are also not the same. What is important here, though, is the relative strength of the four variables in intermarriage.

5. B. B. Wessel, "An Ethnic Survey of Woonsocket, Rhode Island," in Brewton Berry, *Race and Ethnic Relations*, 3d ed. (Boston: Houghton Mifflin Company, 1965), pp. 289-90.

6. We must point out however, that the Warner and Srole formulation was published considerably after the Wessel study.

7. Note that among what is generally considered the most liberal segment of our population, university students, as recently as the early 1960s when Albert I. Gordon's survey was conducted, only 31 percent said that they would marry a Mexican.

8. We have said earlier that the higher the social class, the greater the chance of intermarriage, yet here we pinpoint the lower middle class. This is because there are greater numbers of Chicanos in the lower middle class than in the upper class. The likelihood here is based on absolute numbers rather than on percentages.

5 Intermarriage and Non-Chicanos

Undoubtedly, one can learn much from an analysis of what other groups have experienced with reference to intermarriage. As Donald R. Young states:

> The problems and principles of race relations are remarkably similar, regardless of what groups are involved and . . . only by an integrated study of all minority peoples in the United States can a real understanding and sociological analysis of the involved social phenomena be achieved.[1]

While it will not be possible to analyze completely the situation of other racial and ethnic groups and intermarriage, it is important to look briefly at some intermarriage rates of several racial and ethnic groups in the United States in order to put the Chicano experience into comparative perspective.

The Blacks and Intermarriage

Table 5.1 presents some data on intermarriage rates of the black population. Notice that in this table, with the exception of Hawaii where the number of blacks is very small and where the climate for interracial marriage is unusually favorable, at least 97 percent of blacks who marry, marry other blacks. Note also that there seems to have been been no appreciable increase over time in black-white intermarriage; the New York State rate in the 1920s actually is higher than more current rates in Michigan, California, and Nebraska.

Table 5.1

Rates of Exogamy for Black Individuals
and Marriages, 1921-1964

Area	Period	Percentage of Exogamous Individuals	Percentage of Exogamous Marriages
New York State*	1921-24	3	5
Michigan	1953-63	1	2
California	1955-59	2	4
Hawaii	1956-64	11	20
Nebraska	1961-64	0.3	0.5

*Excluding New York City
Source: Derived from Heer (1966).

Table 5.2 indicates cumulative rates of intermarriage for blacks in the entire nation for the census years of 1960 and 1970.[2] While the percentage of black males who were married exogamously increased somewhat over the ten-year period, the percentage of black females who were outmarried declined slightly. In 1970, approximately one percent of the black married population was intermarried.

Table 5.2
Cumulative Rates of Intermarriage for Blacks
in the United States by Sex, 1960 and 1970

Period	Percentage of Exogamous Males	Percentage of Exogamous Females
1960	0.8	0.8
1970	1.2	0.7
Change Over Time	+0.4	−0.1

Source: Heer (1974), Table 2, p. 248.

Chicano intermarriage rates are considerably higher than black rates of exogamy for reasons based on the differing socio-cultural situations of the two groups. For example, on comparing the situation of blacks and Chicanos in San Antonio, Texas, Bradshaw states:

> Whereas the Negro population is a relatively rigid caste, which is endogamous by legal restrictions, and includes virtually all occupations and institutions necessary to its rather segregated position, the Spanish American population may be said to form a lower class within the white aggregate. The boundaries of this class are clarified and reinforced by physical and cultural difference, as well as economic and social barriers.[3]

According to Myrdal, fear of intermarriage was the rationale used by whites to justify their segregation of blacks.

> The ban on intermarriage has the highest place in the white man's rank order of social segregation and discrimination . . . . No excuse for other forms of social segregation and discrimination is so potent as the one that sociable relations on an equal basis between members of the two races may possibly lead to intermarriage.[4]

That fear of intermarriage with blacks would be so intense as to underpin segregation of the two races seems almost incomprehensible at this time, and yet the final argument justifying the separation of the two groups has been, "But would you want your daughter to marry one?"

St. Clair Drake and Horace R. Cayton believe that there are various types of blacks who intermarry. The types they develop are of interest to us because it is hypothesized that several of them are similar to types of Chicanos who intermarry. The five types of blacks most likely to intermarry, according to Drake and Cayton, are: 1) intellectuals and bohemians; 2) religious and political radicals; 3) members of the "sporting world"; 4) the stable middle class; and 5) the unassimilated foreign-born black unaware of the meaning of intermarriage in the United States.[5] Among Chicanos, this researcher would hypothesize that type 1 (the intellectual part) and type 4 represent the numerical majority of intermarriages. (Interestingly, these two types meet in academia and would suggest that academic Chicanos have a high rate of intermarriage. Currently, though, identification with the Chicano Movement and caution against being labeled a "*vendido*" or "sell out" works against intermarriage of some Chicano academics.)

What are the attitudes of black families and white families in the aftermath of an intermarriage? Joseph Golden's study, done in the late 1940s and early 1950s, shows that white families have little to do with the black individual and tend to shun the couple.[6] Black families, on the other hand, are ready to meet the white partner but not to accept the individual until he or she proves to have some knowledge and appreciation of black culture. Black-white intermarried couples tend to have fewer children than the non-intermarrieds, and the children come to consider themselves black rather than white. The couple, particularly if middle class, tends to live in an integrated neighborhood.

Historically, there have been many instances of black-white intermarriage. Myrdal tells us that Frederick Douglass, nineteenth-century black leader, married a white woman. W. E. B. DuBois, on the other hand, stopped dating a "colored" girl who looked white because too many would think that she was white and that he had married outside of his race.[7] Several Chicano scholars, academicians, and activitists have intermarried, most before they became involved in the Chicano Movement, and many subsequently have divorced, but it is not known to what extent the divorces were the effect of the cultural nationalism and heightened consciousness of the Chicano Movement as opposed to other causes.

Because higher status black males have dated and married white females with greater frequency than white males have dated and married black females, it is not surprising that many black females resent black "brothers" who date or marry whites.[8] The white woman represents competition to black women who are not able to reciprocate the "poaching" because black women rarely are dated by white males.[9] Also, since middle-class black males are in high demand in the black subculture because of their relative economic security and high status, one can see why black females feel strongly about black male-white female interracial dating and marriage.

The White Ethnics and Intermarriage

Table 5.3 is a summary table of past research on some of the white ethnics and their intermarriage rates in one area of the United States. Rates of exogamy for the Italians and Poles in Buffalo were a not inconsiderable 17 per cent and 12 percent respectively as far back as 1930. The rates of outmarriage continue to rise so that by 1960, one-half of all Poles marrying were marrying out, as were more than half of the Italians. As will be shown below, there appear to be many similarities between the trends in the rates of the white ethnics and Chicanos, as well as several important differences.

Table 5.3
Rates of Exogamy for Italian and Polish Individuals
and Marriages, Buffalo, New York, 1930-1960

Period	Percentage of Exogamous Individuals		Percentage of Exogamous Marriages	
	Italians	Poles	Italians	Poles
1930	17	12	29	21
1940	20	16	34	27
1950	36	27	53	43
1952	42	29	59	45
1955	54	45	70	62
1960	56	50	72	67

Source: Derived from Bugelski (1961).

Herbert Gans, in describing the Boston Italian "West Enders," is not too distant from a description of the Chicano dynamic of intermarriage over time.

> Social relationships are almost entirely limited to other Italians, because much sociability is based on kinship, and because most friendships are made in childhood, and thus are influenced by residential propinquity. Intermarriage with non-Italians is unusual among the second generation, and is not favored for the third. As long as both partners are Catholic, however, disapproval is mild.[10]

Notice that by the third generation, ethnicity begins to fade as a major barrier to intermarriage, but that religion remains somewhat important.[11] One can speculate that over a greater amount of time, religion, too, might weaken as an intermarriage barrier, with race and class (future social class) probably remaining longest as significant barriers to general exogamy.[12]

Grebler, et al. feel that Mexican Americans are following in the footsteps of European immigrant groups with reference to marital assimilation. They found an *endogamy* rate of 75 percent for Mexican Americans in Los Angeles in 1963, and in the following quotation compare this with rates of Italians and Polish endogamy reported by Bugelski in Buffalo, New York.[13]

> The 1930 rates of endogamy were 71 per cent for Italians and 79 per cent for Poles, but the 1960 rates were 27 per cent for Italians and 33 per cent for Poles. If one estimates the mid 1890's as the highpoint of Polish and Italian immigration and the 1920's as the crest of Mexican immigration, the 60-70 per cent endogamy rates occurred for both populations approximately 40 years after their highest immigration rates.[14]

Despite similarities, however, the Chicano dynamic differs in certain ways from that of the European immigrants. One major difference is that immigration from Mexico to the United States has not and probably will not decline to the extent that European immigration has declined. Another factor is that the psychology of Chicanos in the Southwest varies from that of European immigrants. Based on a historical awareness that the land was originally Mexican, many Chicanos in the Southwest feel that they are in their homeland rather than in alien territory. Continuing and innumerable border crossings of Mexicans into the United States and of Americans into Mexico along the 1,800-mile border between the United States and Mexico provide a comingling of the groups. The cultural reinforcement of Mexicans in the United States is great, as exemplified by a network of Spanish language television stations in major Southwestern cities as well as by numerous Spanish language radio stations throughout the Southwest.

Japanese and Puerto Rican Intermarriage

Data are available for two other groups: the Japanese, a racial group, and the Puerto Ricans, largely a mixed Caucasian group similar to the Mexican Americans but having substantial numbers of blacks. (See Table 5.4 and 5.5.)

For the Japanese, rates of intermarriage in Los Angeles, California, and in Hawaii were extremely low in the early part of the century, began to rise at mid-century, and by the 1970s involved 31 percent of individuals marrying.

For Puerto Ricans, data are available for New York City, 1949 and 1959. Rates of intermarriage are low when compared to the Italians, Poles, and Japanese for similar years, but they are not as low as black intermarriage rates, again with the exception of Hawaii, for equivalent time periods.

Summary and Conclusion

Rates of intermarriage of groups other than the Mexican Americans were examined in order to put the Chicano experience into perspective.

Table 5.4
Rates of Exogamy for Japanese Individuals
and Marriages, 1912-1972

Area	Period	Percentage of Exogamous Individuals	Percentage of Exogamous Marriages
Hawaii	1912-16	0.3	0.7
Hawaii	1920-34	3	7
Hawaii	1945-54	13	22
Hawaii	1970	31	47
California	1955-59	14	25
Los Angeles	1924-33	1	2
Los Angeles	1949-59	10	19
Los Angeles	1971-72	31	48

Source: Derived from Kikumura and Kitano (1973)

Table 5.5
Rates of Exogamy for Puerto Rican Individuals
and Marriages, New York City, 1949 and 1959

Period	Percentage of Exogamous Individuals	Percentage of Exogamous Marriages
1949	7	13
1959	5	9

Source: Derived from Fitzpatrick (1966).

Black-white intermarriage rates historically have been, and remain, very low. The Drake-Cayton typology of blacks who intermarry was presented, with information on the consequences of black-white intermarriages.

Rates of outmarriage of the Italian and Polish white ethnics turn out to be considerably higher than that of the blacks. Rates for Italians and Poles, high to begin with, show a clear pattern of increase over time. The outmarriage rates of the Japanese have risen over time but have not yet reached the levels of the white ethnics. Puerto Rican intermarriage rates remain low, but not so low as the rates for blacks.

The exact rates of Chicano intermarriage for various times and places will be presented in the next chapter. Let it suffice to say that the rates of Chicano intermarriage, while lower than those of the Italians and Poles in Buffalo, are higher than the black and Puerto Rican rates in the United States.

Notes

1. Quoted in Gunnar Myrdal, *An American Dilemma* (New York: Harper and Brothers, 1944), p. 1185n.
2. A cumulative rate is the percentage of individuals intermarried at some point in time rather than being the percentage of those intermarrying within a given time period (commonly, a year). See Table 6.2 and note 11, p. 69 for parallel information on Chicanos.
3. Benjamin S. Bradshaw, "Some Demographic Aspects of Marriage: A Comparative Study of Three Ethnic Groups" (Master's thesis, The University of Texas at Austin, 1960) pp. 14, 16. The observation must be made, however, that since 1960 the legal barriers placed on black exogamy have been lifted in Texas, and blacks are not as completely segregated occupationally and institutionally as they once were.
4. Myrdal, *An American Dilemma*, p. 606.
5. Cited in Albert I. Gordon, *Intermarriage* (Boston: Beacon Press, 1964), p. 60.
6. Joseph Golden, "Patterns of Negro-White Intermarriage," cited in Albert I. Gordon, *Intermarriage*, p. 264.
7. Myrdal, *An American Dilemma*, p. 1187n.
8. At a shopping center in Austin, Texas, I observed a very well-dressed young black male walking arm in arm with a blonde. Two black girls walking together in the mall noticed the couple and made some remarks between themselves about their "brother" not being a true brother.
9. This seems to be based on sex roles in the United States, in combination with the Western European concept of beauty.
10. Herbert Gans, *The Urban Villagers* (New York: The Free Press, 1965), p. 35.
11. Endogamy by religion is, of course, Kennedy's well-known "triple melting pot" hypothesis. The three "pots" are the three major religious subgroupings in the United States, namely, Protestants, Catholics, and Jews. The hypothesis states that when intermarriage by ethnicity occurs, it occurs *within* rather than *across* the three religious categories.
12. Race as the final barrier in the United States seems to be limited to the Negroid race, however, because Mongoloids, that is, American Indians and Asians, particularly the latter, have increasing intermarriage rates. However, the numbers of Asians in the United States are small and Asians are relatively upwardly mobile, factors conducive to intermarriage and factors which apparently are overriding the variable of race.
13. B. R. Bugelski, "Assimilation Through Intermarriage," *Social Forces*, 40 (December 1961), pp. 148-53.
14. Leo Grebler, Joan W. Moore, and Ralph C. Guzman, *The Mexican American People: The Nation's Second Largest Minority* (New York: The Free Press, 1970), p. 49ln. If we continue with this line of reasoning, by 1990 the projected rate of endogamy for Mexican Americans in Los Angeles will be about 45 percentage points below the 1960 rate, or about 30 per cent. To put this in terms of our preferred statistic, the percentage of individual *exogamy*, the 1990 rate is projected to be about 70 percent. I seriously doubt that the rate will be that high in 1990.

6 Chicano Intermarriage: Other Studies

A History of Chicano Intermarriage

The reenactment of an early California wedding for a Santa Barbara fiesta was reported in the following manner; "A traditional wedding party of 1818 escorted by caballeros, canters along. It represents the wedding of Anita de la Guerra and Capt. Alfred Robinson."[1] This type of wedding sets the tone for much of the early history of Anglo-Chicano intermarriage in the Southwest. Anglo adventurers moving into the Southwest married daughters of the most prominent Hispanic families in the region.

In California, as McWilliams puts it, these men were

> . . . American, British, Scottish, German, and French adventurers who had infiltrated the province prior to 1846. There were only a hundred or so of these adventurers but they played a role of crucial importance at the time of the conquest. With scarcely a single exception, these curiously assorted characters had married daughters of the *gente de razon* after first joining the Catholic Church and accepting Mexican citizenship. Once related to the "best families" by marriage, they became eligible for land grants and were permitted to engage in trade. Embracing the daughters of the land, they also made a pretense of embracing its customs, adopting the prevailing style of dress and Hispanicizing their surnames. At the time of the conquest of course, they went over to the American side en masse and in many cases, induced their in-laws to collaborate with those who were directing the American invasion.[2]

In Texas "as in California, many marriages took place, at an early date, between Anglo-American men and Mexican women in the border counties."[3]

In New Mexico, early Anglo immigration took the same pattern as immigration into the other areas of the Southwest. "Only a hundred or so Anglo-Americans had settled in New Mexico prior to 1846 and most of these had married into prominent 'native' families."[4] In Arizona, we are told that as in the other Southwestern territories there were good relations at first between Americans and Mexicans, and many pioneer Anglo males, founders of families of later prominence, married Mexican women.[5]

To summarize, the picture received of the early period of Chicano-Anglo contact in the Southwest is one in which there is a considerable amount of intermarriage, much of it motivated by the desire of opportunistic Anglo males to marry into the wealthy and well-established Spanish families of the region.

After the conquest and with the coming of the railroads into the Southwest, there was a marked change in Anglo-Mexican relationships. The old Spanish aristocracy, a numerically small part of the Spanish surname population to begin with, was largely eliminated as an important economic and political force. From then on, Anglo Americans clearly played the leading role in the economy of the region. The large majority of Mexicans, working class to begin with, were relegated to the lower socioeconomic positions in the American Southwest.

The new economy provided little opportunity for Chicano upward socioeconomic mobility, and little chance for Anglo-Chicano interpersonal contact and intermarriage. "The basic factor retarding the assimilation of the Mexican immigrant" was "the pattern of his employment."[6] Mexican Americans were to be found working predominantly in seven types of employment: 1) the railroads, 2) smelters, 3) copper mines, 4) sugar beet refineries, 5) farm factories (agribusiness), 6) large fruit and vegetable exchanges, and 7) other large scale industrial enterprises.[7] Such employment required Chicanos to work in all-Mexican work crews or in family units, which resulted in their having very little contact with members of the majority society, other than their bosses. There was little contact with Anglos as social equals, a condition necessary for intermarriage.

In addition, the type of work in which Chicanos were employed often involved being in undesirable isolated locations, such as near mines in the desert or along distant tracts of railroad. Mexican American employment was often seasonal or casual, and jobs frequently were of the dead-end variety. Commonly, Chicanos were employed by highly organized corporations having large capital investments. Such employment offered little opportunity for advancement at the lower levels in which Chicanos were concentrated. All of this resulted in little upward mobility for the Mexican American people and in their having little primary contact with majority members.

Furthermore, "by keeping Mexicans segregated occupationally, employers . . . created a situation in which the skilled labor groups have naturally regarded Mexicans as group competitors rather than as individual employees."[8] Such a situation clearly intensified the amount of prejudice and discrimination directed against the minority by the Anglo majority.

By the 1940s, however, McWilliams noted an increasing number of intermarriages between Anglos and Chicanos not of the elite. As he puts it:

> Originally most of the mixed marriages were between Anglo men and Spanish-speaking women of the *rico* class; but nowadays mixed marriages among the working class are not uncommon as shown by the disconcertingly large number of Carmencita O'Brien's and Juan O'Rourke's to be found in the schools of the larger towns.[9]

Rates of Chicano Intermarriage

Table 6.1 is a summary table of rates of Chicano intermarriage from 1850 to the present in various counties in Texas, New Mexico, Arizona, and California. An analysis of the table reveals several interesting findings. First, the rates of Chicano-Anglo intermarriage vary considerably among the various counties studied. Examining only the time period around 1960, for example, we find that while only 3 percent of all Chicanos marrying in Hidalgo County married exogamously, 25 percent in Los Angeles County married outside of their own group.[10] Grebler, et al., explain why the rate of exogamy for Mexican Americans was higher in Los Angeles than in other areas for comparable time periods.

> Contemporary Los Angeles is far less hostile to Mexican Americans and offers much greater economic opportunity than do most of the other large Southwest metropolitan communities. These features of the external system are apt to affect the boundary maintenance of the ethnic group and facilitate its interaction with the larger community.[11]

For the three states for which sufficient date to make comparisons are available, the highest rates of exogamy occur in California, followed by New Mexico, with the lowest rates being in Texas. Using my preferred statistic, the percentage of exogamous individuals, the highest rate recorded in Texas was 16 percent in Bexar County in 1973. In New Mexico, the highest rate was 31 percent in Bernalillo County in 1967; in California, the highest rate was 38 percent for the entire state in 1962.

In general, there is a clear trend of increasing outmarriage over time. Recently, however, particularly in areas where the highest rates of exogamy have been found (Bernalillo County and the state of California, for example) rates seem to have ceased increasing significantly.

In California, rates of outmarriage increase up to the 1960s and mid-1970s, stabilizing at about 36 percent. In Bernalillo County, New Mexico, the stabilization rate in recent years seems to be about 30 percent, and in Bexar County, Texas, rates do not increase greatly from 1964 to 1973, hovering around 15 percent.

Reasons for the apparent stabilization are unclear. Most likely causal factors are the continuing in-migration from Mexico, and the Chicano Movement of the 1960s and 1970s with its emphasis on ethnic consciousness. However, since the overall trend, as far back as data are available, has been one of slow increase, it is probable that the current stabilization in rates of outmarriage will be temporary and that, as a whole, rates will continue to increase slowly.

Table 6.1
Summary of Studies of Chicano Intermarriage

Researcher	Area	Period	Percentage of Exogamous Individuals	Percentage of Exogamous Marriages
	Texas			
Bean and Bradshaw	San Antonio (Bexar Co.)	1850	5	10
Bean and Bradshaw	San Antonio (Bexar Co.)	1860	5	10
Bradshaw	San Antonio (Bexar Co.)	1940-55	10	17
Bean and Bradshaw	San Antonio (Bexar Co.)	1960	11	20
Murguía and Frisbie	San Antonio (Bexar Co.)	1964	14	24
Murguía and Frisbie	San Antonio (Bexar Co.)	1967	13	23
Murguía and Frisbie	San Antonio (Bexar Co.)	1971	14	24
Murguía and Frisbie	San Antonio (Bexar Co.)	1973	16	27
Alvírez and Bean	Corpus Christi (Nueces Co.)	1960-61	8	15
Alvírez and Bean	Corpus Christi (Nueces Co.)	1970-71	9	16
Alvírez and Bean	Edinburg (Hidalgo Co.)	1961	3	5
Alvírez and Bean	Edinburg (Hidalgo Co.)	1971	5	9
	New Mexico			
Cochrane	Las Cruces (Dona Ana Co.)	1915	0	0
Holscher, et al.	Las Cruces (Dona Ana Co.)	1953	10	18
Holscher, et al.	Las Cruces (Dona Ana Co.)	1967	11	20
Holscher, et al.	Las Cruces (Dona Ana Co.)	1977	15	27

Johnson	Albuquerque (Bernalillo Co.)	1915-16	8	14
Zeleny	Albuquerque (Bernalillo Co.)	1924-40	8	15
Johnson	Albuquerque (Bernalillo Co.)	1945-46	12	22
González	Albuquerque (Bernalillo Co.)	1953	13	23
González	Albuquerque (Bernalillo Co.)	1964	19	33
Murguía and Frisbie	Albuquerque (Bernalillo Co.)	1967	31	48
Murguía and Frisbie	Albuquerque (Bernalillo Co.)	1971	24	39
Holscher, et al.	Seven Counties*	1953	9	16
Holscher, et al.	Seven Counties*	1967	12	22
Holscher, et al.	Seven Counties*	1977	14	24
Arizona				
Stone, et al.	Nogales (Santa Cruz Co.)	1952-62	9	17
California				
Panunzio	Los Angeles (Los Angeles Co.)	1924-33	9	17
Grebler, et al.[10]	Los Angeles (Los Angeles Co.)	1963	25	40
Schoen, et al.	California**	1962	38	55
Schoen, et al.	California**	1966	37	54
Schoen, et al.	California**	1970	36	53
Schoen, et al.	California**	1974	34	51
Burma, et al.	San Bernardino (San Bernardino Co.)	1970-77	34	51

*The seven New Mexican county seats and counties are: Las Cruces (Dona Ana Co.), Roswell (Chavez Co.), Carrizozo (Lincoln Co.), Deming (Luna Co.), Las Vegas (San Miguel Co.), Socorro (Socorro Co.), and Taos (Taos Co.). The rates in this table are the combined rates for all seven counties. Rates for each county for 1953, 1967, and 1977 can be found in Holscher, et al.

**The Schoen, et al., data include the entire state.

Sources: Data adapted from Bean and Bradshaw, 1970 (San Antonio, 1850, 1860, 1960); Bradshaw, 1960 (San Antonio, 1940-55); Murguia and Frisbie, 1977 (San Antonio, 1964, 1967, 1971, 1973; Albuquerque, 1967, 1971); Alvirez and Bean, 1976 (Corpus Christi, 1960-61, 1970-71; Edinburg, 1961, 1971); Gonzalez, 1969 (Las Cruces, 1915; Albuquerque, 1915-16, 1945-46, 1953, 1964); Holscher, et al., 1979 (Las Cruces, 1953, 1967, 1977; Seven Counties, 1953 1967, 1977); Burma, et al, 1979 (San Bernardino, 1970-1977); Stone, et al., 1963 (Nogales, 1952-62); Grebler, et al., 1970 (Albuquerque, 1924-40; Los Angeles, 1924-33, 1963); Schoen, et al., 1978 (California, 1962, 1966, 1970, 1974).

Overall, highly urbanized counties report more intermarriage than do less urbanized counties. In addition, no stabilization has occurred in the less urbanized areas (e.g., see the Holscher, et al., Seven County data); they continue to experience an increase in exogamy. As a result, in recent years there has been somewhat of a convergence of exogamy rates in areas of high population density with those of low density.

Table 6.2 provides additional information concerning Chicano intermarriage. In 1970, 16 out of every 100 currently married Chicano males were married to non-Chicanos. For females, the rate was 17 out of 100. The percentage varies by age, with younger Mexican Americans, both male and female, having higher rates than older Mexican Americans.[12] The fact that younger segments of the Chicano population have outmarried to a greater extent than older segments indicates an assimilative trend.[13]

Table 6.2
Cumulative Rates of Intermarriage for Chicanos
in the United States by Sex and Age, 1970

Age	Percentage of Exogamous Males	Percentage of Exogamous Females
45 and over	12	13
25-44	17	17
16-24	23	21
Total, 16 and over	16	17

Source: *A Study of Selected Socio-Economic Characteristics of Ethnic Minorities, Based on the 1970 Census, Volume I: Americans of Spanish Origin*, Department of Health, Education and Welfare, p. 45.

Summary and Conclusion

In this chapter, a brief discussion of the history of Chicano-Anglo intermarriage described its beginnings in the mid-nineteenth century with Anglo adventurers marrying into the Hispanic aristocracy of the then-Mexican territory. This pattern became rare after the American conquest of the region. Subsequently, Chicano-Anglo intermarriage increased to rates of 16 percent in Bexar County, Texas, in 1973, 31 percent in Bernalillo County, New Mexico, in 1967, and 38 percent in the state of California in 1962.

Although recently rates seem to have stabilized in some areas perhaps as a result of the Chicano Movement and of continuing immigration from Mexico, the overall trend of Chicano intermarriage since the 1850s has been one of slow increase, and it is unlikely that such a trend should radically and permanently change in the future. As of 1970, throughout the United States,

16 percent of all married Mexican American males and 17 percent of all married Mexican American females were married to non-Chicanos.

Part Two of this study turns the focus from a socio-historical description of intermarriage trends to an analysis of variables related to Spanish surname and non-Spanish surname intermarriage.

Notes

1. Carey McWilliams, *North From Mexico* (New York: Greenwood Press, 1968), p. 37.
2. Ibid., p. 90.
3. Ibid., p. 86.
4. Ibid., p. 116. The year 1846 marks the beginning of the war between the United States and Mexico which resulted in the Mexican loss of one-half of its territory, including New Mexico, to the United States.
5. Ibid., p. 124.
6. Ibid., p. 215.
7. Ibid.
8. Ibid., p. 216.
9. Ibid., p. 125. Note that McWilliams uses Irish surnames in his examples. It is likely that intermarriage, particularly in the early decades of this century, when it occurred, took place between the largely Catholic Mexicans and the Catholic Irish and other Catholic ethnic groups. This is consistent with Ruby Jo Reeves Kennedy's "triple melting pot" theory.
10. Commonly, the rate of 25 percent is used for the Mittelbach, et al. study of Los Angeles in 1963, reported in Grebler, et al. However, an examination of the detailed Mittelbach, et al. study (Mexican American Study Project Advance Report 6, pp. 52-58) demonstrates that when methodology similar to that of the Schoen, et al. study is employed, a rate of outmarriage of 39 percent results. The difference between the two rates of 25 percent and 39 percent has to do with the birthplace of Spanish surname individuals marrying. The 39 percent rate includes all Spanish surnames marrying, regardless of birthplace, be it outside the Southwest, or even if it happens to be in another Hispanic nation or commonwealth, such as Cuba or Puerto Rico. The 25 percent rate includes only Spanish surname individuals born in Mexico; born in the United States, one or both parents born in Mexico; or one or both parents with Spanish surnames born within the five Southwestern states. See Mittelbach, et al., pp. 52-58. Probably, the 1963 Los Angeles data slightly underestimate the percentage of Mexican Americans outmarrying while the Schoen, et al. data overestimate the percentage somewhat.
11. Leo Grebler, Joan W. Moore, and Ralph C. Guzman, *The Mexican American People: The Nation's Second Largest Minority* (New York: The Free Press, 1970), p. 407.
12. It should be noted that different means of determining the Mexican American population were used in Tables 6.1 and 6.2. In Table 6.1, based on county and state marriage records, Spanish surnames are used as indicators of Mexican ethnicity. The reliability and validity of this indicator will be discussed in Chapter 7. Table 6.2, from the census, uses the respondents' self-identification of ethnicity. The advantage of using marriage record data for our research problem

is that it can provide a year by year study of rates of intermarriage. In other words, it can provide information on the population *marrying*. Census data can tell us the percentage of Mexican Americans who are intermarried. This will be a cumulative number which will not vary greatly from year to year in any given area. In other words, it provides information only on the currently *married* population, and allows less insight into current rates of intermarriage.

13. Interestingly, this trend is not present in the Puerto Rican population. See *A Study of Selected Socio-Economic Characteristics of Ethnic Minorities, Based on the 1970 Census, Volume I: Americans of Spanish Origin*, Department of Health, Education and Welfare, p. 45. In addition, recent surveys by the Census Bureau seem to indicate that the cumulative percentages of exogamous Chicanos in the United States and in the Southwest have not increased since 1970. The 1976 and 1977 *Current Population Reports* indicate the following:

Cumulative Rates of Intermarriage for Chicanos
In the United States and the Southwest by Sex, 1976 and 1977

	Percentage of Exogamous Males		Percentage of Exogamous Females	
	1976	1977	1976	1977
United States	14.9	15.0	17.3	16.4
Southwest	12.3	11.6	13.4	11.9

Source: U.S. Bureau of the Census, *Current Population Reports*, Series P-20 no. 310, "Persons of Spanish Origin in the United States: March 1976," U.S. Government Printing Office, Washington, D.C., 1977, pp. 42-43, and *Current Population Reports*, Series P-20 no. 329, "Persons of Spanish Origin in the United States: March 1977," U.S. Government Printing Office, Washington, D.C., 1978, pp. 44-45.

The lack of increase in the cumulative rates seems to parallel the apparent stabilization found in the marriage record based data in Table 6.1. Whether the lack of increase in the cumulative rates is real or only statistical, however, remains problematic.

Parenthetically, the above table also indicates that outmarriage for Mexican Americans is greater outside of the Southwest than it is within the Southwest.

PART II
An Empirical Study
of Chicano Intermarriage

7 Data and Methodology

In Part I, intermarriage between minority and majority is considered as the single most conclusive indicator of minority assimilation. Occurrence of large-scale intermarriage indicates the narrowing of social distance between a minority group and the majority, as well as the progressive dissolution of the minority as a distinct and cohesive entity. A high degree of endogamy, on the other hand, indicates the existence of strong social boundaries and the maintenance of ethnic cohesion.

With this chapter, we begin an empirical study of Chicano intermarriage. County marriage records of four counties, Bexar County (San Antonio), Texas; Bernalillo County (Albuquerque), New Mexico; Nueces County (Corpus Christi), Texas; and Hidalgo County (Edinburg), Texas, were collected.[1] All four areas possess important Spanish surname populations.

Table 7.1
Spanish Surname and Total Populations of Bexar,
Bernalillo, Hidalgo, and Nueces Counties, 1970

County	Spanish Surname Population	Total Population	Spanish Surname as Percent of Total
Bexar	308,437	830,460	37.1
Bernalillo	94,233	315,774	29.8
Hidalgo	127,588	181,535	70.3
Nueces	88,339	237,542	37.2

Source: Spanish Surname Population: 1970 Census of Population. Characteristics of Spanish Surname Population by Census Tract. PC(S1)-60 and PC(S1)-61, Table 1. Total Population: 1970 Census of Population. General Social and Economic Characteristics. PC(1)-C33 and PC(1)-C45, Table 43.

San Antonio has the second largest Spanish surname population in the Southwest, second only to Los Angeles. The Spanish surname population is, in part, the result of twentieth-century emigration from Mexico to the United States, stimulated both by the Mexican Revolution of 1910-1930 and by the need for labor in the United States created by the First World War. Ties with Mexico in the Bexar County area have remained close.

Albuquerque possesses the largest Spanish surname population in the northern New Mexico-southern Colorado area. The population of this center traces its origin back to early Spanish settlers who arrived in this region as early as the sixteenth century. For this reason, Spanish surnamed residents of the region often prefer to be called "Hispanos," rather than "Mexican Americans," emphasizing the heritage derived from Spain rather than from Mexico.

Hidalgo County is in the south Texas, lower Rio Grande Valley which borders Mexico.[2] Edinburg (pop. 17,163), although the county seat, is not the only important municipality in the county. In the southern part of the county are a series of towns linked by (and originally established because of) a railroad. These include McAllen (pop. 37,636), Pharr (pop. 15,829), Weslaco (pop. 15,313), Mission (pop. 13,043), and Mercedes (pop. 9,355). The county's industry is noted primarily for its agricultural products, such as citrus fruits, tomatoes, and cotton. The fourth county, Nueces, borders the Gulf Coast of Texas. Its major city, Corpus Christi (pop. 204,525), is an important deep water port.

Characteristics of the Four Counties

While a detailed and comprehensive description of the four counties under study will not be attempted, a brief comparison of the counties will focus on the social distance between Spanish surnames and non-Spanish surnames in each area.

In Hidalgo County, the social distance between Anglos and Chicanos seems to this observer to be the greatest of all of the four counties. The situation here is interesting because Spanish surnames are the numerical majority and non-Spanish surnames sense this danger to their economic and political control. Thus, visible positions of power are often held by Spanish surnames although their actions seem to be dictated by influential Anglos. The standard of living in Hidalgo County is low when compared to other parts of the United States. A mitigating fact might be that Mexico borders the county and that Mexicans there have an even lower standard of living, keeping discontent with extant conditions from spilling over into intense activism.

Nueces County, farther from the Mexican border, is considerably more urban than Hidalgo County. These two elements normally would predict greater political activism on the part of Chicanos since urbanism is less conducive to monolithic control, and distance from the border reduces the feeling of relative prosperity deriving from a comparison of one's standard of living with that of Mexicans in Mexico. Statistically, however, the percentage of Spanish surnames in Nueces County is considerably less than in Hidalgo County, a fact that lessens the political effectiveness of Mexican Americans. Social distance between the Spanish surnamed and non-Spanish surnamed in Nueces County seems to be less than in Hidalgo County, but is greater than in Bexar and Bernalillo counties.

Bexar County has the largest Spanish surnamed population of the four counties surveyed. The absolute'size of this population, as well as its relative size, which approaches parity with non-Spanish surnames in the city of San Antonio, is such that Chicanos in the 1970s and early 1980s began actively to challenge non-Spanish surnames for political leadership of the area. The significantly large Chicano middle class, however, has the tendency to lessen overall social distance and conflict between the minority and the majority.

Bernalillo County, it seems to this observer, has a qualitatively different Spanish surname/non-Spanish surname relationship than do the three Texas counties. The non-Spanish surname population in Bernalillo County, on the whole, seems to have a greater respect and appreciation for Hispanic culture than do the non-Spanish surname populations in the Texas counties. In addition, the presence of the Native Americans as a third group seems to affect and improve relations between Spanish surnames and non-Spanish surnames in New Mexico. Attention is diverted from Anglo-Chicano conflict toward the needs of the numerous poor Native Americans in the region.

The fact that most of the Spanish surnames in New Mexico are not recent migrants from Mexico but have been residents in New Mexico for a long time establishes their primacy, and Hispanic primacy (as well as that of the Native Americans) is recognized by the non-Spanish surnames (although, of course, not entirely).

Subjectively, then, this researcher would rate the social distance of Spanish surnames with non-Spanish surnames as being greatest in Hidalgo County, followed by Nueces County, Bexar County, and finally by Bernalillo County. This ranking, of course, parallels the ranking of the counties as measured by intermarriage (see Table 6.1) with Hidalgo County having the least and Bernalillo County the greatest amount of Mexican American intermarriage.

Data Collection

Data was collected in the counties for the following years: Bexar County 1964, 1967, 1971, and 1973; Bernalillo County 1967 and 1971; Nueces County 1960, 1961, 1970, and 1971; and Hidalgo County 1961 and 1971. As indicated in Chapter 6, San Antonio and Albuquerque had been research sites for previous studies of Anglo-Spanish surname intermarriage (see Table 6.1), so a more recent study of these areas permitted a comparison over time with previously collected information.[3] `

In Albuquerque, two years—1967 and 1971—were sampled. Since the Albuquerque data were collected in 1972, 1971 was selected for analysis, being the latest complete calendar year for which information was available at that time.

One of the original hypotheses guiding data collection was that events collectively referred to as the Chicano Movement, with its emphasis on racial integrity and cultural nationalism[4], would have the effect of depressing rates of Anglo-Chicano intermarriage. The movement gained prominence in New Mexico with what popularly has been called "The Land Grant War of 1967,"[5] led by Reies López Tijerina. The event generating the most interest in New Mexico at that time was a "raid" on the courthouse at Tierra Amarilla in northern New Mexico on June 6, 1967, by Tijerina and his followers.

If one posits that the Chicano Movement first came to the general attention of New Mexicans in 1967, reinforced by the activities in other parts of the Southwest of such leaders as Cesar Chavez in California and Rodolfo "Corky" Gonzáles in Colorado, and allowing approximately a one-year time lag between engagement and marriage, 1968 would be the first year in which the movement might have an effect on rates of intermarriage. Thus, 1967 would have been among the last "pre-Chicano Movement" years. Data previously collected in Albuquerque in 1964 by Nancie L. González supplied relatively recent data useful for trend analysis.

The data for Nueces County and Hidalgo County were collected approximately at the same time as the Bernalillo County data.[6] Since there were no previous studies of intermarriage in Nueces and Hidalgo Counties, a ten-year interval for data collection was chosen. For Nueces County, 1960, 1961, 1970 and 1971 were sampled and for Hidalgo County, 1961 and 1971 were studied.

In San Antonio, the latest available data as well as data comparable to previously collected information were desirable. The years sampled in San Antonio were 1964, 1967, 1971 and 1973. The San Antonio data were collected in the summer of 1974 and so the latest complete calendar year for which marriage applications were available was 1973. The years 1971 and 1967 were sampled to be directly comparable to the Albuquerque data, and 1964 was selected in order to compare it to the González Albuquerque data for that year.

The Samples

Every fifth case in Bernalillo County was selected for inclusion in the sample, resulting in a twenty percent random sample (Total N = 1383).[7] In Bexar County, every tenth case was sampled for the years 1964, 1967, 1971 and 1973 (Total N = 3502). (This sample size is the same as Bradshaw's in his studies of Bexar County marriage application data.) In Nueces County every fifth case was sampled for the years 1960, 1961, 1970, and 1971 (Total N = 2114), although data available for variable analysis (see below) are present only for exogamous marriages in those four years (Total N = 137). In

Hidalgo County, every fifth case was sampled for the years 1961 and 1971 (Total N = 879). For 1961, however, data containing information on variables are available only for the eleven exogamous marriages occurring in that year.

The data for the empirical study of Chicano intermarriage, then, consist of marriage applications dated within the years sampled. From these applications could be derived a total of 28 variables, 6 referring to the marriage itself, 11 to characteristics of the groom and 11 to characteristics of the bride. Appendices A and B contain the list of variables derived from the marriage applications as well as their code value. Because the marriage applications and methodology of data collection were not identical for every county and year sampled, Appendix C is provided to indicate the availability of variables by county and year.

The data collected from marriage applications have the advantage of high reliability and validity. The information asked of individuals was neither of a very personal or sensitive nature, nor was it information which the marriage applicant would have had trouble recalling. The questions are largely of the "name, address, and place of birth" type. The one classification which I had to make on my own, that of determining whether a person was Spanish surnamed or not, was made on the basis of a specific list, the United States Census Detailed List of Spanish Surnames, containing more than eight thousand surnames.

Of course, it is necessary to realize that the correlation between having a Spanish surname and being Mexican American, while very high, is not perfect. Problems with this correlation occur in two different areas. First, there are two other major Spanish surname groups not of Spanish-Mexican heritage in the United States, namely, the Cubans and the Puerto Ricans. These groups do not pose a major difficulty to this study because 1) the population concentrations of these two groups are not in the Southwest, Cubans residing primarily in Florida and Puerto Ricans in the Northeast; and 2) the groups are of rather recent arrival in the United States so that first generation individuals of these two groups can be identified in our data set by place of birth.

Secondly, there are some Mexican origin individuals who, through previous intermarriage, no longer have a Spanish surname. However, a study of population sizes of the peoples in question, employing both the Spanish surname and the self-identification "Mexican Origin" indicator, demonstrates that the Spanish surname and the "Mexican Origin" populations are clearly of the same magnitude in the Southwest,[8] and long term endogamy has, at least until the present, assured a high correlation between ethnicity and surname.

The Study of Anglos and Intermarriage:
  The Breaking of Ties—A Theoretical Framework
  Chapter 6 introduced the discussion of the large-scale trends of Chicano intermarriage as indicated by rates of exogamous individuals and marriages. The study of trends to determine the extent of Mexican American assimilation at present and to ascertain the future of the Mexican American minority as a distinct sociocultural entity were prime motivating factors for data collection. In the process of data collection, the possibility of gathering information on individuals marrying became apparent. Thus, it became of interest to study the characteristics of individuals, both Anglo American and Mexican American, and to establish relationships between these characteristics and exogamy.

  When one begins to analyze the likelihood of majority individuals marrying minority persons, it soon becomes evident that the concept of assimilation is, by itself, insufficient. Assimilation has as its focus changes undergone only by a *minority* over time in its new environmental situation. We must employ a new, even broader concept that will help us understand the likelihood of *majority* members marrying minority individuals. This concept we will call the "breaking of ties." In this way of looking at majority and minority contacts, both minority and majority individuals are seen as being bound by sub-communal ties to generally homogeneous subsystems.[9] The extent to which individuals of each group outmarry will depend on individual characteristics encouraging contact with outgroups.[10]

  When we study individual characteristics, the dependent variable will be exogamy as it has been throughout. The groups analyzed with reference to exogamy will be subdivided by ethnicity and by sex. In other words, the focus will be on four subgroups, namely, Spanish surname males, Spanish surname females, non-Spanish surname males, and non-Spanish surname females. Many, but not all, of the variables will apply to all four subgroups. For example, while the variable of type of ceremony applies to all groups in this study, the variable of civilian or military residence at marriage applies only to males.[11]

The Organization of the Analysis
  In Chapter 8 a detailed examination of what was observed briefly in Chapter 6, namely, the variation in exogamy by county and year, will be presented. Whereas in Chapter 6 we noted that different counties had differing rates of exogamy and that even within counties, rates of outmarriage varied over different years, in Chapter 8 we will incorporate county and year of marriage as independent variables to see how they affect our dependent variable of exogamy.

  Beginning with Chapter 9, we will examine the effect of ten individual characteristics on exogamy. (The eleventh variable, that of month of marriage, was not developed in this study.) Chapter 9 will concern itself with given names and type of ceremony, Chapter 10 with metropolitan or non-metropolitan place of birth, Southwest or non-Southwest place of birth, and generation, Chapter 11 with civilian or military residence at marriage and civilian or military source of identification, and Chapter 12 with sex, age, and divorce. Chapter 13 summarizes the findings of the analysis of the ten variables and returns to our theoretical framework to apply it to the empirical findings in the preceding chapters.

Propositions for the Individual Characteristics Variables

Propositions were developed for the ten individual characteristics variables, the variables which are analyzed in Chapters 9 through 12, as follows:

1) *Given Names:* For Spanish surnamed individuals, those with non-Spanish given names are more likely to marry exogamously than those with undetermined[12] or Spanish given names. Anglicization of given names of Spanish surnamed persons indicates that for those who have non-Spanish given names, some degree of acculturation has taken place. For example, instead of Juan or Juanita González the marriage application might read John or Jane González. Assuming this to be an indication of cultural assimilation, it is hypothesized that the individual with a non-Spanish given name will be more likely to outmarry than an individual who has a Spanish first and/or second given name.

2) *Type of Ceremony:*[13] For the Spanish surnamed, those who choose to marry in a Protestant or a civil ceremony are more likely to marry exogamously than those who marry in a Catholic ceremony. For non-Spanish surnamed individuals, those who marry in a Catholic ceremony are more likely to marry exogamously than those who marry in a Protestant or a civil ceremony. Most Spanish surnamed persons are Catholic and most non-Spanish surnamed individuals are Protestant in the United States. For a Spanish surnamed person to marry in a Protestant ceremony indicates that he or she has had contact with the largely non-Spanish surname Protestant group. On the other hand, for a non-Spanish surnamed individual to marry in a Catholic ceremony indicates either that the person is Catholic, in which case he or she probably is more likely to come into contact with the largely Catholic Mexican American minority,[14] or has come into contact with Catholics.

3) *Metropolitan or Non-Metropolitan Place of Birth:* For all groups, those born in a metropolitan location are expected to show a greater tendency to marry exogamously than those born in a non-metropolitan location. Large urban areas, it is hypothesized, provide greater opportunities for cultural and structural assimilation of minorities, and the social distance between

majority and minority seems to be less in metropolitan as compared to non-metropolitan areas.

4) *Southwest or Non-Southwest Place of Birth:* For non-Spanish surnamed persons, those born out of the Southwest are expected to be more likely to marry exogamously than those born in the Southwest.[15] This is predicted because Anglos from outside the Southwest are likely to have fewer prejudices against the Spanish surnamed than Anglos native to the Southwest where there has been a long history of interethnic conflict. Also, the fact of geographical mobility indicated by a non-Southwestern birthplace may be a sign of breaking of ties.

5) *Generation:* For the Spanish surnamed group, those of the second or later generation are more likely to marry exogamously than those of the first generation. For the Spanish surnamed population, the longer they have resided in the United States, the greater the amount of cultural, structural, and eventual marital assimilation.

6) *Civilian or Military Residence at Marriage* and

7) *Civilian or Military Source of Identification:*[16] Exogamous males, both Spanish surname and non-Spanish surname, will be more likely to have a military residence and/or offer a military source of identification as proof of age than endogamous males. These are the two available indicators of military status and, although they probably underestimate the number of military personnel (e.g., a person in the military could easily live off base and present a drivers license rather than a military identification as proof of age), the two indicators provide us with the first definite empirical evidence on the individual level of the role of the military in exogamy.

Military personnel exemplify the breaking of ties hypothesis very well. They are predominantly young males of marriageable age who are relocated in areas away from home. They most probably will seek out the local female population, be it Spanish surname or non-Spanish surname, for companionship and perhaps for eventual marriage. Thus they are less likely to marry homogamously into their hometown ethnic subcommunities.

8) *Sex:* For Spanish surnames, females are more likely to marry exogamously than males. It has been an almost universal finding in previous studies that Spanish surname females outmarry more than Spanish surname males.[17] There is probably less prejudice and discrimination directed against Spanish surnamed women by the (male dominated) majority society than against Spanish surnamed men.[18] In addition, males ordinarily have had more freedom in mate selection than females and majority males have had more freedom in mate selection than minority males.

9) *Age at Marriage:* For all groups, older individuals are expected to be more likely to marry exogamously than their younger counterparts. An explanation derived from our breaking of ties concept would state that it sim-

ply takes more time for a Spanish surname individual to find a marriage partner outside of his subcommunity. A delay in marriage would result in an increase in chances for exogamy because, at this later date, the ethnic individual may not be associating as exclusively with members of his own ethnicity as earlier in life. Exogamous non-Spanish surnames are more likely to have higher ages at marriage than endogamous non-Spanish surnames because, as we have hypothesized for Spanish surnames, it takes more time to find a suitable marriage partner outside of one's own subsystem than within.

10) *Divorce:* For all groups, it is anticipated that those who have been divorced will be more likely to marry exogamously than those who have not been divorced. A divorce often leads to a severe breaking of ties with those with whom one was previously closely associated. It is more likely to force the individual to form new relationships, perhaps with persons outside his or her subgroup.

Statistical Methods Based on Contingency Tables

In this subsection are described the analytical techniques employed to relate the two contextual variables, county and year, and the ten individual characteristics variables, to exogamy. Traditionally, at least two kinds of statistics have been required in relating variables to one another. First, it must be demonstrated at an acceptable level of probability that a relationship exists. Second, the strength of an association must be ascertained, for with a large sample size, a highly significant relationship may be observed despite a weak association between two variables. Therefore, a second statistic, that of strength of association, must be given.

A standard and useful statistic for determining the existence of an association between two nominal measures at a designated level of significance is chi square (X^2). Additionally, we require a measure of the strength of the association for, as Blalock states, "A difference may be statistically significant without being significant in any other sense."[19] *Phi* ($\emptyset$), a statistic based on chi square,[20] will be employed to measure correlation strengths. *Phi* becomes less useful, however, in larger than two-by-two contingency tables, since for larger tables it can become larger than unity. Therefore, Cramer's V,[21] which yields the same results as *phi* on a two-by-two table, but which is able to handle a larger than two-by-two contingency table, will be used when necessary. Cramer's V varies from 0 to 1, regardless of the size of the matrix, and in essence, this statistic adjusts *phi* for either the number of rows or columns.

In addition, a third useful statistic derived from the contingency tables, Somer's D, will be given.[22] Somer's D has the advantage of indicating the directionality of relationships, i.e., whether a given relationship is positive or negative.

Summary

In this chapter it was indicated that data from four counties containing substantial numbers of Chicanos had been collected. Social distance between Chicanos and Anglos in the four areas was examined, and it was estimated that the relative amounts of social distance in the counties paralleled relative amounts of intermarriage in the four areas.

A rationale for location, time periods, sampling procedures, and the reliability and validity of the data set was provided.

A new theoretical framework designed to expand the concept of assimilation, the breaking of ties, was introduced. This framework refers to the breaking out of generally homogeneous subcommunal social systems by both majority and minority individuals.

Two contextual variables, county and year of marriage, and ten individual characteristics variables to be analyzed in subsequent chapters were presented, and propositions for the individual characteristics variables were introduced. Finally, statistical methods based on contingency tables to be employed in the following chapters were described.

Notes

1. The author is indebted to Professor David Alvírez of Pan American University for the Nueces County and Hidalgo County data, and to Maria Concepción Murguía for assistance in collecting the Bexar County data.
2. This county has been the site of several social scientific studies of Chicanos including Arthur J. Rubel's *Across the Tracks: Mexican Americans in a Texas City* (Austin: the University of Texas Press, 1966) and William Madsen's *Mexican Americans of South Texas* (San Francisco: Holt, Rinehart and Winston, 1964).
3. Some minor differences in data collection and sampling procedures make our study of four counties not perfectly comparable in all respects to previously collected data. Also, as indicated in Table 6.1, rates of exogamy derived from Bernalillo County 1967 and 1971 were first reported in David Alvírez and Frank D. Bean, "The Mexican American Family," in *Ethnic Families in America*, ed. by Charles H. Mindel and Robert W. Habenstein (New York: Elsevier, 1976), p. 285.
4. See Armando B. Rendon, *Chicano Manifesto* (New York: Macmillan, 1971) and Edward Murguía, *Assimilation, Colonialism and the Mexican American People* (Austin: Center for Mexican American Studies, The University of Texas at Austin, 1975).
5. See Richard Gardner, *Grito! Reies Tijerina and the New Mexico Land Grant War of 1967* (New York: Harper and Row, 1971).
6. As mentioned before, the Nueces County and Hidalgo County data were collected by Professor David Alvírez.
7. Although a table of random numbers for the selection of cases was not employed, the sample is essentially random because there is no reason to believe that the assigning of a case number to a couple as they came to apply for a marriage license introduced a systematic bias. Professor González selected all cases for every Monday of the year under study, but this technique seemed to me to have a greater likelihood of introducing bias. For example, one could speculate that exogamous minority individuals would be more likely to obtain marriage applications on Mondays than on other days, because, if we relate exogamy to upward mobility as several researchers have, and if we believe that courting in American society intensifies on the weekend, a greater percentage of exogamous individuals, being ambitious and upward mobile, perhaps might have tended to act on Mondays rather than wait until later in the week.
8. José Hernandez, Leobardo Estrada and David Alvírez, "Census Data and the Problem of Conceptually Defining the Mexican American Population," *Social Science Quarterly*, 53 (March 1973), pp. 671-87.
9. Given our focus, what we mean by homogeneous is simply that Mexican Americans will have primary relationships largely with other Mexican Americans as will Anglo Americans with other Anglos. It is realized that the term "Anglo" is a very broad term, and were I involved in a study of white ethnics in the United States, numerous refinements to the term would have to be made.
10. It should be remembered that some minority members have undergone a considerable amount of cultural assimilation. When this is the case, the *cultural distance* a majority individual has to move in order to be compatible with a minority individual will be minimal. *Social distance* will be determined by the prevailing attitudes of the majority and minority towards each other.
11. Although there were females in the military in our data, the numbers were so small as to preclude meaningful analysis.

12. Undetermined given names are those such as *David* which have the same spelling in Spanish and English.
13. It should be noted that although marriage *application* forms were used in this study, it was possible to ascertain the type of ceremony in which the marriage was performed in the Bernalillo County subsample. In Bernalillo County, the forms allowed for the indication of the church or civil official who witnessed the ceremony, this information being added to the form after the marriage had taken place.
14. This is the "Triple Melting Pot" theory originated by Ruby Jo Reeves Kennedy and developed by Will Herberg. See Ruby Jo Reeves Kennedy, "Single or Triple Melting-Pot? Intermarriage Trends in New Haven, 1870-1940," *American Journal of Sociology*, 49 (January 1944), pp. 331-39, and Will Herberg, *Protestant-Catholic-Jew* (Garden City, New York: Doubleday, 1956).
15. The Southwest is defined as the states of Texas, New Mexico, Colorado, Arizona, and California.
16. The identification was necessary as proof of age.
17. Greater female outmarriage holds as well for Puerto Ricans in New York City and for the Japanese. For the black population, males have outmarried with greater frequency. See Joseph P. Fitzpatrick, "Intermarriage of Puerto Ricans in New York City," *American Journal of Sociology*, 71 (January 1966), pp. 395-406; A. Kikumura and H. L. L. Kitano, "Interracial Marriage: A Picture of the Japanese Americans," *Journal of Social Issues*, 29 (1973), pp. 67-81; David Heer, "Negro-White Marriage in the United States," *Journal of Marriage and the Family*, 28 (August 1966), pp. 262-73.
18. Thus we hear in *Nuestro* magazine, a "thumbs down" to gringos who remark, " 'there's only two things I like about you Mexicans . . . your women and your food.' " *Nuestro*, 2 (August 1978), p. 50.
19. Hubert M. Blalock, *Social Statistics*, 2d ed. (New York: McGraw Hill, 1972), p. 293.
20. It is defined as X^2/N and varies from 0 (no relationship between the two variables), to 1 (a perfect relationship between the two).
21. Cramer's V is defined as
$$\frac{\emptyset}{\min (r\text{-}1),\ (c\text{-}1)}.$$
22. See Norman H. Nie et al., *Statistical Package for the Social Sciences* (New York: McGraw Hill, 1975), p. 299 for a definition of Somer's D. The symmetric version of Somer's D is used in this study.

8 The Contextual Variables: County and Year

In Chapter 6, some information was presented on rates of Chicano exogamy over time for various counties in the United States. In this chapter we will examine more closely those counties and years for which detailed information is available and which are the subject of our own empirical analysis. The counties and years to be studied are: Bexar County 1964, 1967, 1971, 1973; Bernalillo County 1967, 1971; Nueces County 1960, 1961, 1970, 1971; and Hidalgo County 1961, 1971.[1] The total number of marriages in the data set for the above counties and years is 7,883, involving 15,766 individuals.

First, we will look at distributions of endogamous and exogamous marriages by ethnicity for all four counties. Second, concentrating only on the Spanish surname population, four rates of exogamy for each county will be presented. These four are rates of exogamy for marriages, for individuals, for males, and for females. In succession follow tables of statistical tests for relationships involving exogamy and county and, finally, statistical tests for relationships involving exogamy and year of marriage.

Table 8.1 presents data for each of the four counties on the four possible types of inter- and intra-ethnic marriages, namely, the endogamous non-Spanish surname type, the endogamous Spanish surname type, the non-Spanish surname male and Spanish surname female type, and, finally, the Spanish surname male and non-Spanish surname female type. The totals for each county show that the largest divergence in percentages for three of the four types of marriages (the two endogamous types and the non-Spanish surname male, Spanish surname female type) are between Bernalillo County and Hidalgo County. For example, endogamous non-Spanish surname marriages comprise 61 percent of all marriages in Bernalillo County, but only 18 percent in Hidalgo County. For the remaining type, the Spanish surname male and non-Spanish surname female variety, the greatest divergence is between Bernalillo County (7 percent) and Nueces County (2 percent) although the Hidalgo County rate of 2.2 percent is scarcely higher than the Nueces County rate.

The proportions of non-Spanish surname endogamous marriages to all marriages are roughly 60 percent in Bernalillo County, 55 percent in Nueces County, 50 percent in Bexar County, and only 20 percent in Hidalgo County. From these figures we are able to get a sense of the relative size of the non-Spanish surname marrying subpopulations in the four counties. The relative size of the subpopulations, of course, reflects the population composition of the county as a whole (see Table 7.1).

Table 8.1
Endogamous and Exogamous Marriages by Ethnicity

Year	All Classes		Non-SS Male Non-SS Female		SS Male SS Female		Non-SS Male SS Female		SS Male Non-SS Female	
	Number	Percent	Number	Percent	Number	Percent	Number	Percent	Number	Percent
Bexar County (San Antonio), Texas 1964, 1967, 1971, 1973										
1964	612	100.0	323	52.8	218	35.6	45	7.4	26	4.2
1967	787	100.0	421	53.5	282	35.8	53	6.7	31	3.9
1971	996	100.0	475	47.8	397	39.8	65	6.5	59	5.9
1973	1110	100.0	571	51.4	394	35.5	97	8.7	48	4.3
Total	3505	100.0	1790	51.1	1291	36.8	260	7.4	164	4.7
Bernalillo County (Albuquerque), New Mexico 1967, 1971										
1967	604	100.0	380	62.9	117	19.4	69	11.4	38	6.3
1971	781	100.0	470	60.2	189	24.2	63	8.0	59	7.6
Total	1385	100.0	850	61.4	306	22.1	132	9.5	97	7.0
Nueces County (Corpus Christi), Texas 1960, 1961, 1970, 1971										
1960	387	100.0	251	64.8	117	30.2	13	3.4	6	1.6
1961	416	100.0	252	60.6	139	33.4	20	4.8	5	1.2
1970	649	100.0	358	55.2	247	38.0	33	5.1	11	1.7
1971	662	100.0	363	54.8	250	37.8	29	4.4	20	3.0
Total	2114	100.0	1224	57.9	753	35.6	95	4.5	42	2.0
Hidalgo County (Edinburg), Texas 1961, 1971										
1961	296	100.0	81	27.4	204	68.9	8	2.7	3	1.0
1971	583	100.0	74	12.7	466	80.0	27	4.6	16	2.7
Total	879	100.0	155	17.6	670	76.2	35	4.0	19	2.2

Source: Marriage Records, Bexar County, Texas, Bernalillo County, New Mexico, Nueces County, Texas, and Hidalgo County, Texas.

Consistently, Bernalillo County shows higher rates of intermarriage than do the other three counties. In the county which shows the least, Hidalgo County, there is a substantial increase in the percentage of endogamous Spanish surname marriages from 1961 to 1971 (from 69 to 80 percent), whereas the absolute number of endogamous non-Spanish surname marriages actually declines over the same time period (from 81 to 74). Over the 10-year time span, the percentage of exogamous marriages in Hidalgo County greatly increases, although it still remains relatively low.

Notice that in all counties for all years studied the number of non-Spanish surname male-Spanish surname female marriages surpasses those of the Spanish surname male-non-Spanish surname female marriage type. This, of course, means that in all areas Spanish surname females are marrying out in larger numbers than Spanish surname males, a fact that will be analyzed statistically in the subsection on the variable of sex.

Table 8.2 is a major summary table of Chicano intermarriage for the four counties in the years studied. Unlike Table 8.1, it includes information only on marriages which involve the minority; thus, it excludes all endogamous non-Spanish surname marriages.

In Table 8.2, data for single years are combined, giving a summary percentage by county of Chicano exogamy for marriages, individuals, males, and females. From this table, once again it becomes apparent that the New Mexican county (Bernalillo) has by far the greatest amount of outmarriage of the four areas. The three Texas counties follow, with Bexar County exhibiting only slightly more than one-half as much outmarriage as Bernalillo County. Nueces County has approximately one-third the outmarriage of Bernalillo County, while Hidalgo County demonstrates less than one-fifth. In this table, as in Table 8.1, it is very clear that Mexican American females outmarry to a greater extent than do the males, and this finding holds in all four areas.

It should be remembered that in this table, because the years summarized for each county are not identical, the comparison by county is not perfect. For example, although in Bernalillo County the years 1967 and 1971 are combined, in Hidalgo County the years 1961 and 1971 are used. However, if one takes the figures as roughly indicating the 1960-early 1970 time period for the four locations, the major patterns of difference in rates of exogamy in the four places are clear.

County and Exogamy

In Table 8.3 are findings from cross-tabulations on the relationship between county and exogamy; data from three counties for the same year are included. For Spanish surname individuals and for non-Spanish surname males, there are highly significant differences in levels of exogamy among counties (P < .0001). The measure of association (Cramer's V) for Spanish surnames is a substantial .24 for males and .22 for females.

The positive Somer's D's for the Spanish surnamed show that when we move (statistically) from Hidalgo, to Bexar, to Bernalillo Counties, exogamy becomes more likely. For the non-Spanish surname population, the negative Somer's D's indicate a decrease in the probability of exogamy from the first to the third county. Notice that the X^2's, the Cramer's V's and the Somer's D's are considerably smaller for the non-Spanish surnamed than for the Spanish surnamed, and that for Anglo females the X^2 is not significant even at the .05 probability level.

Table 8.2
Endogamous and Exogamous Marriages of Mexican Americans

	Total	Endo-gamous	Exogamous	Exogamous as Percent of Total
Bexar County 1964, 1967, 1971, 1973				
Number of Marriages Involving Mexican Americans	1715	1291	424	24.7
Number of Individuals	3006	2582	424	14.1
Number of Males	1455	1291	164	11.3
Number of Females	1551	1291	260	16.8
Bernalillo County 1967, 1971				
Number of Marriages Involving Mexican Americans	535	306	229	42.8
Number of Individuals	841	612	229	27.2
Number of Males	403	306	97	24.1
Number of Females	438	306	132	30.1
Nueces County 1960, 1961, 1970, 1971				
Number of Marriages Involving Mexican Americans	890	753	137	15.4
Number of Individuals	1643	1506	137	8.3
Number of Males	795	753	42	5.3
Number of Females	848	753	95	11.2
Hidalgo County, 1961, 1971				
Number of Marriages Involving Mexican Americans	724	670	54	7.4
Number of Individuals	1394	1340	54	3.9
Number of Males	689	670	19	2.8
Number of Females	705	670	35	5.0

Source: Table 8.1

Table 8.3
Statistical Tests for Relationships
Involving Exogamy and County
by Sex and Ethnicity

Bexar County 1971, Bernalillo County 1971, Hidalgo County 1971

| Sex and Ethnicity | N | Measure of Significance | | | Measure of Association | Measure of Directionality |
		X^2	df	P	Cramer's V	Somer's D[1]
SS Male	1186	70.46	2	.0001	.24	+.20
Non-SS Male	1174	17.66	2	.0001	.12	−.06
SS Female	1207	57.80	2	.0001	.22	+.18
Non-SS Female	1153	3.60	2	.1649	.06	−.02

[1]A plus (+) Somer's D indicates an increase in the likelihood of exogamy from Hidalgo, to Bexar, to Bernalillo counties; a minus (−) indicates a decrease in the likelihood of exogamy.

The importance of statistically significant differences in rates of exogamy by county can scarcely be overemphasized. Areas in the Southwest clearly differ with reference to the Chicano/Anglo interpersonal dynamic, certain areas being more open to the development of primary type relationships between the two groups and others being more closed. These statistics reflect the culmination of local historical developments in combination with demographic and socioeconomic realities.

Year and Exogamy

Table 8.4 demonstrates that, with one exception, there has been no statistically significant change in the amount of outmarriage over time in Bernalillo County and in Bexar County for the years indicated.

This reiterates in a more detailed manner what was indicated in Chapter 6, namely, that although there has been an increase in Chicano exogamy in the United States over the long run, the trend toward increasing exogamy has been slow to develop and, in fact, in recent times there seems to have been a stabilization in the rates of outmarriage in some areas, particularly those previously experiencing relatively high rates of exogamy.

In Bernalillo County, the trend may have experienced a slight reversal due, perhaps, to minority militant activities at the time and to a change in the (largely non-Spanish surname) military population stationed in the area. This change may have affected marriage rates of Spanish surname females, the only group to experience a significant decline in outmarriage from 1967 to 1971.[2]

Looking closely at Table 8.4, in Bexar County note that there was no significant change in exogamy from 1964 to 1973 for all four groups,

Table 8.4

Statistical Tests for Relationships
Involving Exogamy and Year of Marriage
by Sex and Ethnicity

Sex and Ethnicity	N	Measure of Significance			Measure of Association Phi	Measure of Directionality Somer's D[1]
		N^2	df	P		
Bexar County 1964, 1973						
SS Male	686	.002	1	.9632	.00	+.00
Non-SS Male	1036	.87	1	.3511	.03	+.03
SS Female	754	.62	1	.4309	.03	+.03
Non-SS Female	968	.00	1	.9639	.01	+.01
Bernalillo County 1967, 1971						
SS Male	403	.002	1	.9633	.01	−.01
Non-SS Male	982	2.34	1	.1261	.05	−.05
SS-Female	438	6.87	1	.0087	.13	−.13
Non-SS Female	947	.87	1	.3517	.03	+.03

[1]A plus (+) Somer's D indicates an increase in the likelihood of exogamy over time; a minus (−) indicates a decrease in the likelihood of exogamy.

although the positive Somer's D's indicate that what little change that did occur was in the direction of increased exogamy. In Bernalillo County, the direction of change was toward decreased exogamy for Spanish surname persons of both sexes, for non-Spanish surname males, and, as previously noted, significantly so for Spanish surname females (P < .01). Only the non-Spanish surname female category experiences a slight but non-significant increase in exogamy over time.

Summary and Conclusion

In this chapter, numbers and percentages of endogamous and exogamous marriages in Bexar, Bernalillo, Nueces, and Hidalgo Counties for the 1960-early 1970 time period were presented. Bernalillo County was identified as having the highest rates of exogamy of the four counties, followed by Bexar, Nueces and Hidalgo Counties, in that order. Spanish surname females were shown to have higher rates of outmarriage than Spanish surname males.

On examining the effect of our contextual variables, county and year, on exogamy, two important findings became clear. First, overall, there were shown to be large and significant differences among rates of Chicano intermarriage in different areas. Secondly, no significant increases in outmarriage were found over a four-year time span in Bernalillo County, nor over a nine-year time period in Bexar County. Lack of significant increases in these two areas during the time periods studied could reflect that, overall, the trend line of Chicano exogamy has increased only slowly over time. Also, the data was collected during a time of increased ethnic awareness which may have contributed to a lack of significant increase.

Notes

1. As indicated in Appendix C, data available for Nueces County (all years) and for Hidalgo County 1961 are more limited than data for other counties and years.
2. See Chapter 11 for the effect of the military on intermarriage. A military base in the county was closed during the 1967-1971 time period, although with no over-all loss of military personnel in the area. The closure, however, may have disrupted established patterns of interaction between military personnel and the local Spanish surname female population.

9   The Variables of Given Names and Type of Ceremony

In this chapter, the relationship between exogamy, our dependent variable, and two independent variables, given names and type of ceremony will be studied. These two variables, the first of the ten individual characteristics variables to be analyzed, turn out to be among the best predictors of exogamy of the variables available to this study.

Given Names and Exogamy

Table 9.1 provides information on the ethnicity of given names, by sex, for the Spanish surnamed population marrying in Bexar County in 1964, 1967 and 1971. Names clearly Spanish are ones such as "Miguel"; names such as "Michael" were classified as clearly non-Spanish. The undetermined category refers to names that have the same spelling in Spanish and in English, such as "Daniel."

For Spanish surnamed males, an assimilative trend away from Spanish first given names and toward increasing percentages of non-Spanish or English first names is clearly discernible. Second given names tend to remain considerably more Spanish than first given names, although, even here, a clear movement toward Anglicization can be noted.[1] In general, patterns similar to those for males are present for Spanish surname females. As with Spanish surname males, there are increasing numbers of non-Spanish first and second given names for females over time, and second given names remain more Spanish than first given names. The undetermined category for both males and females is larger for first given names than for second given names, and there seems to be an increase, although not a monotonic increase, in the undetermined category over time. Male first given names are less Spanish and second given names are more Spanish than female given names. One reason that a greater percentage of second, or middle, names remain Spanish than first given names is that second names are sometimes family names. An example of this would be a name such as John *Ortiz* González.

The undetermined category is of particular interest because it can be considered a neutral or "compromise" category of names. Names in this cateogry satisfy both cultures, and an increase in the number of given names in this category may be seen as an attempt on the part of the Spanish surname minority to adjust to the often contradictory demands of two cultures. Since the first given name is used in everyday life to a greater extent than the sec-

Table 9.1

Ethnicity of Given Names, Spanish Surname Individuals
Bexar County 1964, 1967, 1971

	Clearly Spanish		Clearly Non-Spanish		Undetermined	
Year	Number	Percent	Number	Percent	Number	Percent
Male First Given Names						
1964	170	71.1	53	22.2	16	6.7
1967	204	67.1	86	28.3	14	4.6
1971	277	61.0	136	30.0	41	9.0
Total	651	65.3	275	27.6	71	7.1
Male Second Given Names						
1964	125	88.6	15	10.6	1	0.7
1967	138	84.7	24	14.7	1	0.6
1971	170	79.8	37	17.4	6	2.8
Total	433	83.8	76	14.7	8	1.5
Female First Given Names						
1964	186	73.8	29	11.5	37	14.7
1967	219	67.2	61	18.7	46	14.1
1971	287	63.2	84	18.5	83	18.3
Total	692	67.0	174	16.9	166	16.1
Female Second Given Names						
1964	120	83.9	21	14.7	2	1.4
1967	121	72.9	37	22.3	8	4.8
1971	157	65.7	66	27.6	16	6.7
Total	398	72.6	124	22.6	26	4.7

ond given name, it receives a greater amount of exposure to the conflicting demands of the two cultures. (In fact, most frequently second names are simply initialed rather than written out in full.) This is perhaps why there are more undetermined names among first given names than among second given names.

It may be that males have a higher percentage of non-Spanish first given names than females because Spanish surname males must work harder at being accepted by the majority society than Spanish surname females. One way of minimizing differences between themselves and the majority society is for Spanish surname males to adopt English given names.[2] Also, it is probably more acceptable for Spanish surname females to retain their ethnic names without sanction in American society than for Spanish surname males to do so.[3]

Table 9.2 provides evidence of a positive and significant relationship between exogamy and non-Spanish given names for male first and second given names and female first given names. The relationship, however, is not significant for female second given names at the .05 level.

When we look only at first given names, the measure of association is larger for males than for females. The strongest relationship between Spanish surname male exogamy and non-Spanish given names is for second given names, which has a Cramer's V of .27 as opposed to a Cramer's V of .18 for first given names. Thus our proposition stated in Chapter 7 positing a positive relationship between non-Spanish given names and exogamy is largely confirmed.

Table 9.2
Statistical Tests for Relationships
Involving Exogamy and First and Second Given Names[1]
by Sex and Ethnicity

Bexar County 1964, 1967, 1971

		First Given Names				
		Measure of Significance			Measure of Association	Measure of Directionality
Sex and Ethnicity	N	X^2	df	P	Cramer's V	Somer's D
SS Male	997	34.13	2	.0001	.18	+.16
SS Female	1032	7.11	2	.0286	.08	+.07
		Second Given Names				
SS Male	517	38.05	2	.0001	.27	+.26
SS Female	548	5.54	2	.0627	.10	+.08

[1]Given names were placed in three categories: clearly Spanish, undetermined, and clearly non-Spanish.

[2]A plus (+) Somer's D indicates an increase in the likelihood of exogamy from clearly Spanish to undetermined to clearly non-Spanish given names; a minus (−) indicates a decrease in the likelihood of exogamy.

Type of Ceremony and Exogamy

Data were available for the type of ceremony in which a marriage was performed in Bernalillo County; Table 9.3 is a frequency distribution of the types of ceremonies performed in that county in 1967 and 1971 by marriage type. There are clear differences between endogamous non-Spanish marriages and endogamous Spanish surname marriages by type of ceremony. Only 15 percent of endogamous non-Spanish marriages were Catholic over the two years studied as compared to 62 percent of endogamous Spanish sur-

Table 9.3
Type of Ceremony
Bernalillo County 1967, 1971

Year	Catholic		Jewish		Protestant		Civil	
	Number	Percent	Number	Percent	Number	Percent	Number	Percent
Endogamous Non-Spanish Surname Marriages								
1967	59	16.5	5	1.4	206	57.5	88	24.6
1971	62	13.8	2	0.4	291	65.0	93	20.8
Total	121	15.0	7	0.9	497	61.7	181	22.4
Endogamous Spanish Surname Marriages								
1967	66	58.9	0	0.0	6	5.4	40	35.7
1971	114	63.7	0	0.0	11	6.1	54	30.2
Total	180	61.8	0	0.0	17	5.8	94	32.3
All Exogamous Marriages								
1967	49	47.6	0	0.0	13	12.6	41	39.8
1971	35	30.4	0	0.0	41	35.7	39	33.9
Total	84	38.5	0	0.0	54	24.8	80	36.7

Table 9.4

Type of Ceremony of Exogamous Marriages

Bernalillo County 1967, 1971

Year	Catholic		Jewish		Protestant		Civil	
	Number	Percent	Number	Percent	Number	Percent	Number	Percent
Non-Spanish Surname Males and Spanish Surname Females								
1967	27	40.9	0	0.0	7	10.6	32	48.5
1971	21	35.0	0	0.0	21	35.0	18	30.0
Total	48	38.1	0	0.0	28	22.2	50	39.7
Spanish Surname Males and Non-Spanish Surname Females								
1967	22	59.5	0	0.0	6	16.2	9	24.3
1971	14	25.5	0	0.0	20	36.4	21	38.2
Total	36	39.1	0	0.0	26	28.3	30	32.6

name marriages. On the other hand, only 6 percent of endogamous Spanish marriages were Protestant, as opposed to 62 percent of endogamous non-Spanish surname marriages. Slightly more endogamous Spanish surname marriages were performed in a civil ceremony (32.3 percent) than were endogamous non-Spanish surname marriages (22.4 percent).

When we look at intermarriages, we find that the percentages of Catholic and of Protestant marriages fall between the percentages found in the two endogamous marriage types. For example, while 15 percent of endogamous non-Spanish surname marriages and approximately 62 percent of endogamous Spanish surname marriages were performed in a Catholic ceremony, about 39 percent (a percentage in between the two other rates) of intermarriages were performed in a Catholic service. However, the percentage of civil ceremonies for exogamous marriages (36.7 percent) is greater than either the percentage of civil ceremonies for endogamous Spanish surname marriages (32.3 percent) or for endogamous non-Spanish surname marriages (22.4 percent). A civil ceremony may be serving as a compromise type of ceremony, chosen if the two individuals marrying are of different religions. This may explain the relatively high percentage of civil ceremonies among exogamous marriages, assuming that Spanish surnames are largely Catholic and that non-Spanish surnames are largely Protestant.

Within categories of marriage types and ceremony types, two changes over the two years are particularly noteworthy. One is a marked increase of exogamous marriages taking place in a Protestant ceremony from 1967 (12.6 percent) to 1971 (35.7 percent). A second is a decline in the frequency of civil ceremonies for all types of marriage.

Since exogamous marriages are of two kinds, it is possible to analyze them separately, and Table 9.4 is provided for this purpose. The major difference between the two types of exogamous marriages is that the Spanish surname male-non-Spanish surname female type of exogamous marriage has a higher percentage of marriages taking place in a Protestant ceremony (28.3 percent) than the non-Spanish surname male-Spanish surname female type of exogamy (22.2 percent). This may indicate the influence of the Anglo female on the selection of the type of ceremony.[4]

Interestingly, the non-Spanish surname male-Spanish surname female type of marriage has a greater percentage not of Catholic, but of civil ceremony marriages. We can speculate that the influence of the majority male may be so great that the Spanish surname female does not insist on a Catholic ceremony, but compromises with a civil ceremony.[5]

Table 9.5 provides the results of statistical tests of relationships between exogamy and type of ceremony.[6] In Chapter 7 we proposed that for Spanish surnames, marriage in a non-Catholic ceremony would be related to exogamy and that for non-Spanish surnames, marriage in a Catholic ceremony

Table 9.5

Statistical Tests for Relationships
Involving Exogamy and Type of Ceremony
(Catholic, Civil, Protestant)
by Sex and Ethnicity

Bernalillo County 1967, 1971

| Sex and Ethnicity | N | Measure of Significance | | | Measure of Association | Measure of Directionality |
		X^2	df	P	Cramer's V	Somer's D[1]
SS Male	383	37.70	2	.0001	.31	+.24
Non-SS Male	925	74.67	2	.0001	.28	−.24
SS Female	417	32.33	2	.0001	.28	+.24
Non-SS Female	891	46.58	2	.0001	.23	−.19

[1]A plus (+) Somer's D indicates an increase in the likelihood of exogamy from Catholic to civil to Protestant; a minus (−) indicates a decrease in the likelihood of exogamy.

would be related to exogamy. The relations proposed are confirmed by Table 9.7 in the directions hypothesized at a high level of significance ($P < .0001$) and at a moderate level of strength (Cramer's V's from .23 to .31).

Summary and Conclusion

In this chapter, two variables, given names and type of ceremony, were studied and their relationship to exogamy examined. For Spanish surnames, there was a trend over time toward increasing percentages of English first and second given name. Second given names remained more Spanish than first names, perhaps because second names receive less exposure in daily life. Undetermined given names (names with the same spelling in Spanish and English), were seen as compromise names, names acceptable to both cultures. Relationships between non-Spanish given names and intermarriage were statistically confirmed.

As expected, endogamous non-Spanish surname marriages tended to be performed in Protestant ceremonies while endogamous Spanish surname marriages tended to take place in Catholic ceremonies. Civil ceremonies were seen, in part, as compromise ceremonies. Highly significant relationships were demonstrated between exogamy and ceremony type for all four categories of individuals.

Notes

1. There are current tendencies away from Anglicization among some in the Mexican American population, however. In a recent issue of a popular magazine for Latinos, *Nuestro*, individuals "who use an Anglo first name, instead of their Latino name, when they converse or write" were given a "thumbs down." *Nuestro*, 2 (April 1978), p. 80.

2. Note that an English given name can be given to a Spanish surname individual at birth by his parents, or an individual himself may get into the habit of using the English form of his Spanish given name. An English given name, this researcher believes, is an indication of a desire to gain acceptability in the eyes of the majority society, either on the part of parents who gave their child an English name, or on the part of one who uses the English form of his Spanish name.

3. The reason for this is perhaps that females in American society are seen as embodying home and tradition, that is, the expressive rather than the instrumental side of our social system. The value of ethnic cultures, when any value at all is recognized by the majority, is seen to lie in the expressive rather than in the instrumental sphere. This results in an ethnic name being less sanctioned if it belongs to a female than if it belongs to a male. A female with an ethnic name is often seen as traditional, that is, less liberated, more pliable, and, therefore, less of a threat to extant sex role definitions. (Interestingly, with the advent of the Chicano Movement, however, an ethnic name for a female may indicate not traditionality and pliability, but an ethnically conscious and perhaps a feministically conscious, individual.)

4. It is realized that some of the discussion concerning type of ceremony and exogamy concerns not how religion may affect the likelihood of exogamy, but rather, once exogamy is in the offing, how ethnicity affects the choice of ceremony. This is due to the fact that the data indicate not the religious affiliation of the individuals involved, but rather, the type of ceremony in which the marriage was performed. The original direction of the hypothesis can be maintained, however, if we assume that most Spanish surnamed individuals are Catholic, and that most non-Spanish surnamed persons are non-Catholic.

5. Historically, the Roman Catholic clergy has been forbidden to officiate at any mixed marriage without conversion of the non-Catholic or at least with an agreement on the part of the non-Catholic to raise the children as Catholics. These restrictions have been relaxed somewhat in recent time.

6. As indicated in Table 9.5, there were only a total of seven Jewish marriages for the two years studied, and these occurred within the endogamous non-Spanish surname marriage category. Being so few in number, they were not included in the crosstabulation analysis.

10 The Variables of Metropolitan or Non-Metropolitan Place of Birth, Southwest or Non-Southwest Place of Birth, and Generation

In this chapter, we will investigate three variables based on the place of birth of individuals marrying as indicated on their marriage application forms. The variable of metropolitan or non-metropolitan place of birth applies to both Spanish surname and non-Spanish surname persons. Southwestern or non-Southwestern place of birth will apply only to non-Spanish surnames, and the variable of generation, that is, being born in Mexico (first generation), or being born in the United States (second or later generation), applies only to Spanish surnames.

Metropolitan or Non-Metropolitan Place of Birth

By a metropolitan place of birth is meant a place of birth located within a Standard Metropolitan Statistical Area as defined by the United States Census in 1970.[1] Appendix D is a list of the Standard Metropolitan Statistical Areas in Texas and in New Mexico. Since there was but one SMSA in New Mexico in 1970 (Albuquerque), a person born in New Mexico was considered as having a metropolitan birthplace if born in the Albuquerque SMSA and non-metropolitan if born elsewhere in the state. Only those born in Texas were included in the metropolitan/non-metropolitan analysis of Bexar County and Hidalgo County, and only those born in New Mexico were included in the Bernalillo County analysis.[2] Table 10.1 is a frequency distribution of metropolitan or non-metropolitan place of birth for Spanish surname and non-Spanish surname males and females, by county and by marriage type.

This table demonstrates that overall approximately two-thirds of all individuals marrying report a metropolitan place of birth. Those marrying in Bexar County are most likely to have had an urban birthplace, followed by those marrying in Bernalillo County and Hidalgo County, in that order. Females have a slightly higher percentage of metropolitan birthplace than males, and non-Spanish surnames tend to have been born in urban localities to a greater extent than Spanish surnames. In Hidalgo county, there is a relatively high percentage[3] of non-Spanish surname females with a metropolitan place of birth.

Table 10.1

Metropolitan or Non-Metropolitan Place of Birth
Bexar County[1] 1967, 1971, 1973; Bernalillo County[2] 1967, 1971;
Hidalgo County[1], 1971

County	Metropolitan		Non-Metropolitan	
	Number	Percent	Number	Percent
Spanish Surname Males				
Bexar	778	81.1	181	18.9
Bernalillo	171	51.4	162	48.6
Hidalgo	111	38.4	178	61.6
Total	1060	67.0	521	33.0
Non-Spanish Surname Males				
Bexar	605	70.9	248	29.1
Bernalillo	135	61.4	85	38.6
Hidalgo	19	38.8	30	61.2
Total	759	67.6	363	32.4
Spanish Surname Females				
Bexar	892	81.3	205	18.7
Bernalillo	202	55.5	162	44.5
Hidalgo	116	36.9	198	63.1
Total	1210	68.2	565	31.8
Non-Spanish Surname Females				
Bexar	735	75.4	240	24.6
Bernalillo	166	58.7	117	41.3
Hidalgo	27	56.3	21	43.8
Total	928	71.1	378	28.9

[1]Includes only those born in Texas
[2]Includes only those born in New Mexico

Table 10.2 is a summary table of statistical tests for metropolitan/non-metropolitan place of birth and exogamy. It is clear from this table that while metropolitan place of birth is significantly related to exogamy for females, both Spanish surname ($P < .05$) and non-Spanish surname ($P < .001$), such is not the case for males.

A reason for the non-significance of the relationship for males could be that non-metropolitan born individuals subsequently moved into metropolitan areas and have taken on characteristics of those living in urban areas. We know that they have moved into metropolitan areas (at least temporarily) because the counties in which their marriages are registered, Bexar, Berna-

Table 10.2
Statistical Tests for Relationships
Involving Exogamy and Metropolitan or Non-Metropolitan
Place of Birth by Sex and Ethnicity

Bexar County 1967, 1971, 1973
Bernalillo County 1967, 1971
Hidalgo County 1971

Sex and Ethnicity	N	Measure of Significance			Measure of Association	Measure of Directionality
		X²	df	P	Phi	Somer's D[1]
SS Male	1581	0.01	1	.9422	.0002	−.0002
Non-SS Male	1122	0.28	1	.5968	.02	+.02
SS Female	1775	5.79	1	.0161	.06	+.06
Non-SS Female	1306	10.53	1	.0012	.09	+.09

[1]A plus (+) Somer's D indicates an increase in the likelihood of exogamy from non-metropolitan to metropolitan place of birth; a minus (−) indicates a decrease in the likelihood of exogamy.

lillo and Hidalgo, are themselves within SMSAs. The geographical mobility of an individual may indicate a non-typical non-metropolitan born person, which fact may be blurring hypothesized metropolitan/non-metropolitan differences. A better test of our hypothesis that metropolitan life is more conducive to intermarriage than non-metropolitan life, unavailable to us in our data, would involve the inclusion of non-metropolitan individuals who married in non-metropolitan areas into our analysis.

Southwest or Non-Southwest Place of Birth, Generation and Exogamy

This section deals with two variables, Southwest or non-Southwest place of birth and generation, both variables based on the regions where marrying individuals were born. The regions for Spanish surname individuals are Mexico, the Southwest, and the non-Southwest.[4] The regions for non-Spanish surnames are the Southwest and the non-Southwest.

For non-Spanish surnames, as indicated by the variable's name, those born outside of the Southwest are compared with those born in the Southwest. For Spanish surnames, those born in Mexico, that is, first-generation individuals, are compared with those born in the United States, i.e., those of second or later generation.

Tables 10.3 and 10.4 are frequency distributions of the place of birth of the marrying populations of the three counties, Table 10.3 indicating the birthplace of the Spanish surname population and Table 10.4 specifying birthplaces of the non-Spanish surname group.

Table 10.3

Birthplace of Spanish Surname Individuals
Bexar County 1967, 1971, 1973; Bernalillo County 1967, 1971;
Hidalgo County 1971

County	Mexico		The Southwest[1]		Non-Southwest	
	Number	Percent	Number	Percent	Number	Percent
Spanish Surname Males						
Bexar	161	13.3	973	80.4	76	6.3
Bernalillo	10	2.5	378	93.8	15	3.7
Hidalgo	153	31.7	311	64.5	18	3.7
Total	324	15.5	1662	79.3	109	5.2
Spanish Surname Females						
Bexar	123	9.5	1109	86.1	56	4.3
Bernalillo	10	2.3	403	92.0	25	5.7
Hidalgo	144	29.3	333	67.7	15	2.8
Total	277	12.5	1845	83.2	96	4.3

[1]Texas, New Mexico, Colorado, Arizona, California.

In Table 10.3, about 15 percent of Spanish surnames marrying are first-generation individuals, about 80 percent were born in the Southwest, and the remaining 5 percent were born outside of the Southwest.

On comparing counties, Hidalgo County, reflecting its proximity to the border, has a much higher percentage of persons born in Mexico than the other two counties. The percentage of individuals marrying in Hidalgo County born in Mexico is almost three times higher than in Bexar County and is more than ten times higher than in Bernalillo.

A slightly greater percentage of males are of the first generation than females; on the other hand, more females than males report a Southwestern place of birth. Since the marriage took place in the Southwest, the larger percentages of places of birth outside of the Southwest for males is indicative of a greater geographical mobility on their part.

In Table 10.4, about one-half of the non-Spanish surname male marrying population was born in the Southwest. (In the two Texas counties, about 55 percent had a birthplace in the Southwest while in Bernalillo, roughly 40 percent had a Southwestern birthplace.) By comparison, about 60 percent of non-Spanish surname females marrying had a Southwestern birthplace. Similar to what was indicated concerning the Spanish surname group, the lower percentage of Southwestern birthplace of non-Spanish surname males demonstrates their greater geographical mobility when compared to their female counterparts.

Table 10.4
Birthplace of Non-Spanish Surname Individuals
Bexar County 1967, 1971, 1973; Bernalillo County 1967, 1971;
Hidalgo County 1971

County	The Southwest		Non-Southwest	
	Number	Percent	Number	Percent
Non-Spanish Surname Males				
Bexar	932	55.4	750	44.6
Bernalillo	411	41.9	570	58.1
Hidalgo	54	54.0	46	46.0
Total	1397	50.6	1366	49.4
Non-Spanish Surname Females				
Bexar	1037	64.6	568	35.4
Bernalillo	486	51.3	461	48.7
Hidalgo	53	63.1	31	36.9
Total	1576	59.8	1060	40.2

In striking contrast to the Spanish surname population where only about 5 percent were born in the non-Southwest (other than Mexico), about 45 percent of non-Spanish surnames were so born.

Among the counties, Bernalillo had the highest percentages of non-Southwestern birthplaces, reflecting the relatively large influx of non-Spanish surnames from areas outside of the Southwest into that county.

Table 10.5 presents results of statistical tests for relationships between exogamy and Southwest or non-Southwest place of birth for non-Spanish surnames. For males, the relationship is in the hypothesized direction, that is, non-Southwest place of birth is positively related to exogamy, but the relationship is not statistically significant. For non-Spanish surname females, the relationship is significant but in the direction opposite that hypothesized. In other words, non-Spanish surname females born in the Southwest are more likely to outmarry than those born outside of the Southwest. It could be that proximity, that is, growing up with and going to school with Spanish surname persons, particularly those of the same social class, may be responsible for this negative relationship. For non-Spanish surname females, proximity could be cancelling out our hypothesized non-Southwest non-prejudice toward Spanish surnames.[5] Also, non-Southwest born Anglo females marrying in the Southwest could already have been engaged to marry their immigrating (or, perhaps, military) non-Spanish surname males back home, thus not really having been "at risk" in the Southwest.

Table 10.5

Statistical Tests for Relationships
Involving Exogamy and Southwest or Non-Southwest Place of Birth
by Sex and Ethnicity

Bexar County 1967, 1971, 1973
Bernalillo County 1967, 1971
Hidalgo County 1971

Sex and Ethnicity	N	Measure of Significance X^2	df	P	Measure of Association Phi	Measure of Directionality Somer's D[1]
Non-SS Male	2671	.67	1	.4130	.02	+.02
Non-SS Female	2518	9.19	1	.0024	.06	−.05

[1]A plus (+) Somer's D indicates an increase in the likelihood of exogamy from Southwest to non-Southwest place of birth; a minus (−) indicates a decrease in the likelihood of exogamy.

For Spanish surnames, Table 10.6 demonstrates that there is a statistical relationship between being of second or later generation and exogamy. The relationship is slightly stronger for females than for males and is as proposed in Chapter 7.

Table 10.6

Statistical Tests for Relationships
Involving Spanish Surname Exogamy and Generation
by Sex and Ethnicity

Bexar County 1967, 1971, 1973
Bernalillo County 1967, 1971
Hidalgo County 1971

Sex and Ethnicity	N	Measure of Significance X^2	df	P	Measure of Association Phi	Measure of Directionality Somer's D
SS Male	2068	11.21	1	.0008	.08	+.08
SS Female	2198	8.12	1	.0044	.06	+.06

[1]A plus (+) Somer's D indicates an increase in the likelihood of exogamy from first generation to second and later generations; a minus (−) indicates a decrease in the likelihood of exogamy.

Summary and Conclusion

This chapter, has investigated the relationship between three variables, all based on birthplace, and intermarriage. Metropolitan or non-metropolitan place of birth referred to whether or not an individual was born in a Standard Metropolitan Statistical Area. There were statistically significant relationships between being born in a metropolitan area and exogamy for both Spanish surname and non-Spanish surname females. The relationship did not hold for males, however.

For non-Spanish surnames, a Southwest or a non-Southwest place of birth was related to exogamy. The relationship was significant only for females, but in a direction opposite that hypothesized. That is, non-Spanish surname females born in the Southwest were *more likely* to intermarry than those born outside of the Southwest.

Finally, as expected, second, and later generation Spanish surname males and females were more likely to intermarry than were first-generation Spanish surnames.

Notes

1. The fact that some of these areas may not have been designated as SMSA's when the individuals were born does not seem to pose a serious problem. It is highly unlikely that population change in the 20-25 year range (the time period from birth to marriage for most), would have blurred out basic rural-urban dichotomy for most areas.
2. Information concerning metropolitan or non-metropolitan place of birth is limited to those born in-state because in the transcription of the marriage applications only the state in which the person was born was recorded for individuals born outside of the state in which the data were being collected. For those born in state, the town or city as well as the state was recorded.
3. Compared to the other three categories of individuals marrying in Hidalgo county.
4. The Southwest is defined as the five states of Texas, New Mexico, Colorado, Arizona, and California.
5. Also, it really doesn't take long to pick up an ethnic prejudice.

11 Military Status and Chicano Intermarriage

The effect of military status on Chicano intermarriage was first indicated in a study by Benjamin S. Bradshaw;[1] his awareness of this factor most probably stemmed from the fact that the time period he chose to study, 1940-1955, included two major wars, and the area he was studying, Bexar County (San Antonio), Texas, was the location of numerous military installations. According to Bradshaw, "Though less apparent for the years of the Korean War than for World War II, periods of warfare have a definite influence on the extent of exogamy, and thus expedite assimilation."[2]

In Bradshaw's study, the year (1943) for which he recorded the greatest amount of exogamy in Bexar County was also one of the most important years of World War II in terms of the numbers of Americans in the military.[3] During times of war, greater numbers of minority and majority individuals in the military resulted in a greater amount of intergroup contact and, subsequently, in an increase in outmarriage.

Little tells us that "historically, no provision was made for family life within the military community. The recruitment base was typically young, unmarried men."[4] It is not unreasonable to surmise that as these young, single men were assigned to posts far from home, they would attempt to come into contact with the local female population, with some such contact leading to intermarriage. This military structure, which largely recruits young single men and relocates them away from home, represents one of the basic reasons for the relationship between military status and outmarriage.

In addition, Bradshaw believed that wartime was conducive to exogamy "not only because of a large influx of military personnel, but also because of a relaxing of norms governing exogamy."[5]

As Table 11.1 indicates, marriage in the military varies by rank, and, by clear inference, age. San Antonio, Texas, the area studied by Bradshaw and one of the two areas examined in this chapter has an overabundance of military personnel in the lower ranks. In fact, one of the five major military installations in the area, Lackland Air Force Base, is the location of basic training for the Air Force both at the enlisted and officer levels.

In 1968, approximately 76 percent of officers and 42 percent of enlisted men in the armed forces were married.[6] As previously indicated, age greatly influences the rate of marriage and many unmarried enlisted men are those just entering the service, large numbers of whom do not reenlist. It seems clear, then, that the military does provide a continuing supply of young marriageable men available to local populations of women.

Table 11.1

Percent Married Military Personnel by Rank and Branch of Service, 1965

Grade	Army	Navy	Air Force
Enlisted:			
E1, E2	21.1	8.0	12.8
E6	88.1	86.0	90.0
Officers:			
Second Lieutenant/Ensign	51.0	38.0	38.2
Major/Lieutenant Commander	95.4	93.0	95.0

Source: Little, "The Military Family," p. 250.

There are indirect indications that it is probably the enlisted men who intermarry with minority (in this case, Mexican American) females. According to Little, "there is a higher degree of normative regulation of marital choice among officers than enlisted men. Enlisted men are three times as likely to be married to foreign-born wives (20.3 percent) as compared to commissioned officers (6.2 percent)."[7] Although Mexican American females may or may not be foreign-born, if we make an association (often made in the United States and which has had a historical basis in fact) between minorities in the United States and "foreigners," Little's data becomes relevant. Foreign-born women, like minority women in the United States, rank low in status, and status differences between ethnic women and enlisted men are less than those between ethnic women and officers.

The very fact that Little equates normative regulation with low rates of foreign-born wives indicates the relatively low status of foreign-born women. When intermarriage occurs, the exchange seems to be that American military men are attracted to foreign-born women's subservience, while the women are attracted to the men's relatively greater affluence.[8] Hypothetically, at least, a similar exchange exists between Anglo military males and Mexican American females. For intermarriage between Anglo females and Chicano males, the exchange is that the Chicano male enjoys the Anglo woman's higher status because of her caste, and the women is attracted to the Chicano male's at least equivalent if not superior class standing.[9]

The case must not be overstated, however, for as Little points out, "military personnel are often viewed as transients with whom persisting relationships are futile."[10] This view of the military by the non-military works against intermarriage. On the other hand, the stigmatization of military status by the civilian population is likely greatest among the civilian upper-middle and upper social classes. It would not be as great among lower status populations, and a large number of Mexican Americans would have to be so classified.

A Common Enemy and Intermarriage

Earlier it was indicated that Bradshaw believed exogamy to be expedited during wartime because of a relaxation of norms affecting intermarriage. One of the major findings of W. L. Warner et al. in "Jonesville" during World War II was exactly this. They say,

> In wartime internal antagonisms are drained out of the group onto the common enemy . . . . The local ethnic groups, too frequently excluded from participation in community affairs, are given an honored place in the war effort, and the symbols of unity, rather than the separating differences, are stressed . . . . Those who believe that the war's hatreds can bring only evil to our psychic life might well ponder the therapeutic and satisfying effect on the minds of people who are turning their once private hatreds into social ones and joining their townsmen and countrymen in this basic emotion.[11]

Differences are put aside and commonalities are stressed because there is a common enemy. Also, there is a possibility that people may want a respite from internal strife and internal problems; an external threat gives them the rationale to do so.

From still another source, there seems to be some justification for the assertion of a relaxation of internal discrimination during times of conflict with an outside enemy. In a well-known study, Muzafer Sherif and his associates demonstrated that an outside enemy can bring conflicting elements of an entity together.[12] Moskos, as well, has addressed the issue of common danger and its effect on intergroup relations. In referring to how relations between blacks and whites in the military work better under certain circumstances than under others, he says, "The social contact must take place under conditions of equal status and in which mutual interdependence is required for unit cohesion." He goes on to say that the clearest example of a situation containing these elements is "in the actual combat situation where close living, strict discipline, and *common danger*[13] all serve to preclude social conflict between whites and blacks."[14]

War results in a de-emphasis in social background, more particularly in a de-emphasis in class or ethnic differences because of the commonality of the opposing danger.[15] The newspaper in "Jonesville" during World War II, as described by Warner et al., is a good example of the de-emphasis of class and ethnicity.

> Any friend or relative could use this medium [a newspaper column for information about service men] to inform the community at large concerning his "Service Man's" latest move by calling the *Jonesville Eagle* office. Although personals and society news tend to be limited to the middle and upper class, this column included items running from the

very top to the very bottom of the social scale. The armed forces included men from all parts of the community, and it was popularly assumed that the past made no difference as they were all fighting for the common cause.[16]

Some of the data analyzed in this book was collected during the war in Vietnam. Granted that there were vast differences in civilian and military morale and attitudes between World War II and Vietnam, there were some similarities. Since minority individuals serve disproportionately in the armed forces, prejudice and discrimination against them was considered somewhat hypocritical. The argument is that if they were good enough to fight for the nation, they should be good enough to marry anyone in the nation.

Socioeconomic Mobility and Intermarriage

Along with a direct decrease in the amount of prejudice and discrimination, there exists another latent function of wartime, one not unrelated to a decrease in prejudice and one most important for minorities and other disadvantaged groups, namely, increased opportunities for upward mobility. Warner et al. referring to the effect of World War II on American society in general and "Jonesville" in particular, state, "Upward economic mobility increased tremendously in amount and speed; women advanced to jobs never before available to them, ethnic and racial groups raised the ceiling on their job expectations, unskilled workers learned new skills."[17]

In and of itself, upward mobility on the part of a minority is a good indicator of diminishing social distance between it and the majority. Additionally, in the United States upward mobility historically has lead to increased contact between minority and majority individuals.

Two Indicators of Military Status

From the data, it was possible to derive two indicators of military status. On the marriage application form, the applicant was asked to indicate his or her current place of residence. (The number of *females* reporting a military residence was so small as to preclude any meaningful statistical analysis.) Civilian or military place of residence, then, is our first indicator of military status. Secondly, on the form some proof of age was required, indicating that the individual was of legal age to marry. This usually took the form of a birth certificate, a driver's license, or a military identification card. If the latter was presented, the individual was classified as having a military source of identification. Once again, the numbers of females presenting military identification cards were so small as to preclude analysis.

An individual could have either or both a military residence at marriage and a military source of identification, and although there was some overlap, the two variables were analyzed separately.

Civilian or Military Residence at Marriage and Exogamy

Unlike the Bradshaw data which involved the size of a military population in an area, in our data we are able to identify individuals in the military and study the relationship between military status and exogamy.

Table 11.2 is a frequency distribution of civilian or military residence at marriage for Spanish surname and non-Spanish surname males in Bexar and Bernalillo Counties by type of marriage. Note that in 1967, the year for which comparable data are available, Bernalillo County has slightly smaller percentages of both Spanish surname and non-Spanish surname military men than does Bexar County for the same year.

For non-Spanish surname males there is a pattern of declining percentages of individuals of military status over the nine year period. For Spanish surname males, no clear patterns over time is exhibited; overall, about two per-

Table 11.2
Male Civilian or Military Residence at Marriage by Sex and Ethnicity
Bexar County 1964, 1967, 1971, 1973; Bernalillo County 1967

Year	Civilian		Military	
	Number	Percent	Number	Percent
	Spanish Surname Males			
	Bexar County			
1964	235	97.1	7	2.9
1967	303	96.8	10	3.2
1971	455	99.8	1	0.2
1973	431	97.5	11	2.5
Total	1424	98.0	29	2.0
	Bernalillo County			
1967	150	97.4	4	2.6
	Non-Spanish Surname Males			
	Bexar County			
1964	304	82.8	63	17.2
1967	415	87.6	59	12.4
1971	488	90.4	52	9.6
1973	624	93.4	44	6.6
Total	1831	89.4	218	10.6
	Bernalillo County			
1967	397	88.6	51	11.4

Table 11.3

Statistical Tests for Relationships Involving Exogamy and Male Civilian
or Military Residence at Marriage by Sex and Ethnicity

Bexar County 1964, 1967, 1971, 1973
Bernalillo County 1967

| Sex and Ethnicity | N | Significance | | | Association | Directionality |
		X²	df	P	Phi	Somer's D¹
SS Male	1607	5.41	1	.0201	.06	+.05
Non-SS Male	2497	4.55	1	.0329	.04	+.04

¹A plus (+) Somer's D indicates an increase in the likelihood of exogamy from civilian to
military residence; a minus (−) indicates a decrease in the likelihood of exogamy.

cent were of military status compared to over ten percent of non-Spanish
surname males of similar status.

Importantly, Table 11.3 demonstrates that exogamy is associated with
military residence at marriage to a statistically significant degree ($P < .05$) for
both Spanish surname and non-Spanish surname males. The relationship is
slightly stronger for Spanish surname males than it is for the non-Spanish
surnamed.

Civilian or Military Source of Identification and Exogamy

Table 11.4 is a frequency distribution of civilian or military source of identification for Spanish surname and non-Spanish surname males in Bexar
County by year and marriage type. Table 11.4 indicates a decline in percentages of military status males of both the minority and the majority since
1967. Similar to what was found in Table 11.2, there is a much greater
overall percentage of non-Spanish surname males in the military as compared to the percentage of minority males of this status.

The results of a statistical analysis of these data are presented in Table
11.5. In this table, we see that the relationship between a military source of
identification and exogamy for Spanish surname males is similar to the relationship between exogamy and military residence at marriage for Spanish
surname males; that is, it is significant and positive. The relationship
between military source of identification and exogamy for non-Spanish surname males, although positive, while not statistically significant at the .05
level, is in the proposed direction.

Table 11.4

Male Civilian or Military Source of Identification by Sex and Ethnicity
Bexar County 1967, 1971, 1973

Year	Civilian		Military	
	Number	Percent	Number	Percent
	Spanish Surname Males			
1967	275	87.9	38	12.1
1971	434	95.2	22	4.8
1973	413	93.4	29	6.6
Total	1122	92.7	89	7.3
	Non-Spanish Surname Males			
1967	357	75.3	117	24.7
1971	462	85.6	78	14.4
1973	558	83.5	110	16.5
Total	1377	81.9	305	18.1

Table 11.5

Statistical Tests for Relationships Involving Exogamy and Male Civilian or
Military Source of Identification by Sex and Ethnicity

Bexar County 1967, 1971, 1973

Sex and Ethnicity	N	Measure of Significance			Measure of Association	Measure of Directionality
		X^2	df	P	Phi	Somer's D[1]
SS Male	1211	4.86	1	.0276	.07	+.07
Non-SS Male	1682	2.60	1	.1066	.04	+.04

[1]A plus (+) Somer's D indicates an increase in the likelihood of exogamy from civilian to military source of identification; a minus (−) indicates a decrease in the likelihood of exogamy.

Summary and Conclusion

This chapter has examined the relationship between exogamy and military status for Spanish surname and non-Spanish surname males. Two indicators of military status were used, namely, residence at marriage and source of identification.

Military residence at marriage was found to be related to outmarriage to a statistically significant degree for both Spanish surname and non-Spanish surname males. Additionally, a significant relationship was demonstrated between exogamy and military source of identification for Spanish surname males. For non-Spanish surname males, the relationship between a military source of identification and intermarriage, although positive, was not statistically significant.

There are good indications, then, that there is a relationship between exogamy and military status for Spanish surname males. Our results for non-Spanish surname males, while not as conclusive as the findings for minority males, are highly suggestive of a similar positive relationship.

Notes

1. Benjamin S. Bradshaw, "Some Demographic Aspects of Marriage: A Comparative Study of Three Ethnic Groups" (Master's thesis, The University of Texas at Austin, 1960).
2. Ibid., p. 59.
3. Ibid., p. 51.
4. Roger W. Little, "The Military Family," in *Handbook of Military Institutions*, ed. by Roger W. Little (Beverly Hills: Sage Publications, 1971), p. 247. Although in this quotation, Little is referring to American military forces in the nineteenth century, conditions have not changed to the present.
5. Bradshaw, "Some Demographic Aspects of Marriage," p. 51.
6. Little, "The Military Family," p. 249.
7. Ibid., p. 253.
8. R. Druss, "Foreign Marriages in the Military," *Psychiatrics Quarterly*, 39, pp. 220-26.
9. There are indications that Anglo females who intermarry may be of a relatively low social class standing. One indirect indication of this is their young age at marriage. See the information presented on age at marriage in the following chapter.
10. Little, "The Military Family," p. 26.
11. W. Lloyd Warner and Associates, *Democracy in Jonesville* (New York, Harper and Brothers, 1949), p. 288.
12. Muzafer Sherif, et al., "Experiments in Group Conflict," *Scientific American*, 195 (1956), pp. 54-58, and Muzafer Sherif et al., *Intergroup Conflict and Cooperation: The Robbers Cave Experiment* (Norman, Oklahoma: The University of Oklahoma Book Exchange, 1961).
13. My emphasis.
14. Charles C. Moskos, Jr., "Minority Groups in Military Organization," in *Handbook of Military Institutions*, op. cit., p. 282. Recent racial strife between blacks and whites in the military in Germany is related to the fact that the troops are prepared for but are not actually engaged in real combat. Much effort must be expended to keep these troops busy.
15. Even the caste-like distinctions between officers and enlisted men seem to be reduced in wartime.
16. Warner et al., *Democracy*, p. 271
17. Ibid., p. 268.

12 The Variables of Sex, Age, and Divorce

This chapter will deal with the final three variables, sex,[1] age, and divorce, and, as throughout this study, relate them to our dependent variable of exogamy. All three turn out to be significantly related to intermarriage for at least some of our four marrying subgroups.

Sex and Exogamy

A universal finding in the study of Chicano intermarriage is that Spanish surname females tend to marry exogamously more frequently than Spanish surname males. By looking at Tables 8.1 and 8.2 (Chapter 8), it is clear that this study confirms previous findings. Invariably, for every year studied in all four counties, exogamous marriages of the non-Spanish male-Spanish surname female type were greater in number than those of the Spanish surname male-non-Spanish surname female type. It should be noted, however, that neither in this nor in previous studies is the differential between the two types of exogamous marriages extremely large.

Table 12.1 shows us the overall relationship between exogamy and sex for Bexar, Bernalillo, and Hidalgo counties. The positive Somer's D for Spanish surnames indicates that Spanish surname females are more likely to outmarry than Spanish surname males; this relationship is highly significant (P < .0001). For non-Spanish surnames, the negative Somer's D indicates that non-Spanish surname males are more likely to outmarry than non-Spanish surname females. This relationship, too, is highly significant (P < .0001). For both Spanish surnames and non-Spanish surnames, the direction of the relationship between exogamy and sex is as was predicted in Chapter 7.

Age and Exogamy

Table 12.2 presents mean ages at marriage by sex and ethnicity for the three counties for which there were available data.

Upon analyzing mean ages, note that in all three counties Spanish surname males have a younger average age at marriage than non-Spanish surname males, and Spanish surname females marry at a younger age on average than do non-Spanish surname females. These differences in mean ages at marriage probably reflect differences in class standing between the two populations. For the non-Spanish surnames, those marrying in Bexar County had the lowest mean age at marriage, followed by Bernalillo and Hidalgo Counties in that order. For the Spanish surnames, the lowest mean age was in Bernalillo County, followed by Bexar and Hidalgo Counties.

Table 12.1

Statistical Tests for Relationships Involving
Exogamy and Sex by Ethnicity

Bexar County, 1964, 1967, 1971, 1973
Bernalillo County 1967, 1971, Hidalgo County 1971

Ethnicity	N	Measure of Significance X^2	df	P	Measure of Association Phi	Measure of Directionality Somer's D[1]
Spanish Surnames	4814	24.96	1	.0001	.07	+.07
Non-Spanish Surnames	6132	25.90	1	.0001	.06	−.06

[1]A plus (+) Somer's D indicates an increase in the likelihood of exogamy from male to female; a minus (−) indicates a decrease in the likelihood of exogamy.

Table 12.2

Mean Age At Marriage by Sex and Ethnicity

Bexar County 1964, 1967, 1971, 1973
Bernalillo County 1967, 1971
Hidalgo County 1971

Non-Spanish Surname Males	Spanish Surname Males	Non-Spanish Surname Females	Spanish Surname Females
	Bexar County		
26.7	24.6	24.0	22.8
	Bernalillo County		
27.4	24.3	24.9	22.3
	Hidalgo County		
33.5	26.1	28.6	23.6

Hidalgo County exhibits a strikingly high mean age at marriage when compared to the other two counties, especially for the non-Spanish surnames (the differential between the mean age in Hidalgo and Bernalillo for non-Spanish surname males is 6.1 years). The reason for the very high mean age at marriage in Hidalgo County is not known.

In Table 12.3 we test for relationships between exogamy and age at marriage. While the relationship for males, both Spanish surname and non-Spanish surname, is not significant, significant relationships do exist between exogamy and age at marriage for non-Spanish surname females (P < .001) and for Spanish surname females (P < .0001). The direction of the relationship between exogamy and age at marriage for Spanish surname and non-Spanish surname females is not the same, however. For Spanish surname females, older ages at marriage are related to exogamy; for non-Spanish surname females younger ages are related to outmarriage.

Table 12.3

Statistical Tests for Relationships Involving
Exogamy and Age[1] at Marriage by Sex and Ethnicity

Bexar County 1964, 1967, 1971, 1973
Bernalillo County 1967, 1971
Hidalgo County 1971

| Sex and Ethnicity | N | Measure of Significance | | | Measure of Association | Measure of Directionality |
		X^2	df	P	Cramer's V	Somer's D[2]
SS Male	2338	5.58	2	.0614	.05	+.01
Non-SS Male	3125	0.34	2	.8435	.01	−.01
SS Female	2479	26.62	2	.0001	.10	+.08
Non-SS Female	2985	15.01	2	.0006	.07	−.05

[1]Age categories are 1-19, 20-24, 25 +.

[2]A plus (+) Somer's D indicates an increase in the likelihood of exogamy from the first (youngest) age category, to the second category, to the third; a minus (−) indicates a decrease in the likelihood of exogamy with age.

While the finding of a positive and significant relationship between an older age at marriage and exogamy for Spanish surname females is as expected, the finding that younger non-Spanish surname females are more likely to intermarry than their older counterparts is contrary to what was theorized. It could be that young non-Spanish surname females are less tradition-bound than older non-Spanish surname females and consider ethnicity a less serious barrier to marriage. We will examine this and other variables whose relationships were not as predicted for the non-Spanish surname female group in the final chapter of this study.

Divorce and Exogamy

The variable of divorce is available for Bexar County 1971 and 1973 and for Hidalgo County 1971. It is also available in Bexar County 1967, but for females only. Tables 12.4 and 12.5 are frequency distributions of divorce by sex, ethnicity, county, and year.

In Table 12.4, we find that Spanish surname males have considerably lower percentages of divorce as compared to the non-Spanish surnames, in both Bexar and Hidalgo counties. In fact, the divorce rate in Hidalgo County in 1971 for Spanish surnames is only about one-fourth that of the non-Spanish surnames for the same county and year. The percentage of divorced individuals in Bexar County increased from 1971 to 1973 for both the Spanish surname and non-Spanish surname male groups.

Table 12.4

Male Previous Divorce

Bexar County 1971, 1973
Hidalgo County 1971

Year	Not Divorced		Divorced	
	Number	Percent	Number	Percent
Non-Spanish Surname Males				
Bexar County				
1971	412	76.6	126	23.4
1973	478	71.6	190	28.4
Total	890	73.8	316	26.2
Hidalgo County				
1971	79	79.0	21	21.0
Spanish Surname Males				
Bexar County				
1971	402	88.4	53	11.6
1973	380	86.0	62	14.0
Total	782	87.2	115	12.8
Hidalgo County				
1971	456	94.6	26	5.4

Patterns similar to those exhibited in Table 12.4 can be found in Table 12.5, which concerns itself with marrying females and previous divorce. There is an increase in the percentage of previously divorced individuals for both non-Spanish surname and Spanish surname females over time in Bexar County. Rates for divorced Spanish surname females are lower than rates for the non-Spanish surnames and rates in Hidalgo County are lower than those in Bexar County. Additionally, a comparison of Tables 12.4 and 12.5 reveals that the percentages of previously divorced females of both ethnicities for all years and areas are less than the percentages of divorced

males. Part, at least, of the differences in divorce between the Spanish surnamed and the non-Spanish surnamed has to do with the fact that the Mexican American population is largely Catholic while the majority population
is largely non-Catholic.

Table 12.5
Female Previous Divorce

Bexar County 1967, 1971, 1973
Hidalgo County 1971

Year	Not Divorced		Divorced	
	Number	Percent	Number	Percent
Non-Spanish Surname Females				
Bexar County				
1967	367	81.2	85	18.8
1971	433	81.1	101	18.9
1973	466	75.3	153	24.7
Total	1266	78.9	339	21.1
Hidalgo County				
1971	79	87.8	11	12.2
Spanish Surname Females				
Bexar County				
1967	317	94.6	18	5.4
1971	405	87.7	57	12.3
1973	413	84.1	78	15.9
Total	1135	88.1	153	11.9
Hidalgo County				
1971	473	96.1	19	3.9

Table 12.6 summarizes the relationships involving exogamy and previous
divorce. This table shows the relationships are statistically significant only for
females. Note, however, that the direction of the relationship is positive for
Spanish surname females, indicating that a previous divorce increases the
likelihood of exogamy, while for non-Spanish surname females, a negative
relationship indicates that previous divorce decreases the likelihood of outmarriage. This finding for non-Spanish surname females is contrary to
what we hypothesized and will be dealt with at greater length in the final
chapter of this study.

Table 12.6

Statistical Tests for Relationships Involving
Exogamy and Previous Divorce by Sex and Ethnicity

Bexar County, 1967[1], 1971, 1973
Hidalgo County 1971

Sex and Ethnicity	N	Measure of Significance			Measure of Association	Measure of Directionality
		X^2	df	P	Phi	Somer's D^2
SS Male	1380	0.00	1	.9832	.01	−.01
Non-SS Male	1306	1.17	1	.2788	.03	−.03
SS Female	1780	4.67	1	.0308	.05	+.05
Non-SS Female	1694	4.64	1	.0313	.06	−.05

[1]Note that the Bexar 1967 subfile contains only female divorce information.

[2]A plus (+) Somer's D indicates an increase in the likelihood of exogamy from not divorced to divorced; a minus (−) indicates a decrease in the likelihood of exogamy.

Summary and Conclusion

In this chapter, we have looked at the relationships between exogamy and three individual characteristics variables: sex, age at marriage, and previous divorce. We found that, invariably, Spanish surname females marry out to a greater degree than do Spanish surname males, and correspondingly non-Spanish surname males marry out more than do non-Spanish surname females. With reference to age at marriage, there were significant relationships between this variable and females only. For Spanish surname females, a high age at marriage was related to exogamy while for non-Spanish surname females, a low age at marriage was so related. Finally, there was significant relationships between exogamy and previous divorce for females only. The relationship was positive for Spanish surname females, but negative for non-Spanish surname females. The fact that younger, not previously divorced Anglo females are more likely to outmarry was not as predicted, and these anomalous findings will be examined at greater length in the final chapter of this study.

Notes

1. In the original coding of the data, as indicated in Codebook I (Appendix A), information on males and females is available but there is no variable of sex itself. A new file was created which enabled us to analyze the variable of sex, and Codebook II (Appendix E) describes this file.

13 Conclusion

This chapter will first summarize the analysis of the individual characteristics variables which have been discussed in Chapters 9 through 12. Next, returning to my theory of breaking of ties, it will study in particular those variables whose relationships to exogamy were not as predicted, specifically with reference to non-Spanish surname females. A typology of resulting intermarriage life-styles will be developed and, finally, the future of Chicano intermarriage will be studied to ascertain what possible direction Anglo/Chicano relations may take.

Summary of Individual Characteristics Variables

Table 13.1 is a summary table of the ten individual characteristics variables for Spanish surname males, non-Spanish surname males, Spanish surname females, and non-Spanish surname females. Four pieces of information are given for each variable by subgroup: 1) the significance of the relationship at a given level of probability, 2) the strength of the relationship as indicated by Phi or Cramer's V, 3) the direction of the relationship based on the Somer's D statistic, and 4) whether or not the direction of the relationship was as proposed in Chapter 7 where hypotheses concerning the variables and intermarriage were presented.

Of the 23 instances in which a variable was significant for a subgroup, 20 were in the direction predicted. The strengths of the relationship were greatest for type of ceremony for all four subgroups, followed by given names for Spanish surname males. The variable of age for non-Spanish surname females also had a Cramer's V of at least 10.

Statistically significant at the .001 level (or greater) were the following variables: type of ceremony for all four groups, sex for all four groups, age for the two female groups, first and second given names for Spanish surname males, and generation for Spanish surname males.

Thus, the empirical study has demonstrated that several variables, such as type of ceremony, sex, and generation have a significant effect on exogamy. Some new variables from county marriage applications were developed, such as given names and civilian or military residence at marriage. Also, that most of the relationships found in the empirical study were in the direction hypothesized gives me confidence that the theoretical approach was valid.

Breaking of Ties

In Chapter 7, the discussion included a concept of breaking of ties, in which both minority and majority individuals were seen as being bound by subcommunal ties to generally homogeneous subsystems. In subsequent chapters, it was demonstrated that several individual characteristics variables, indicators of breaking of ties and of contact[1] with an outgroup, were related to exogamy.

Several differences in emphasis became apparent when I began to study the characteristics of majority individuals with reference to exogamy instead of concentrating exclusively on minority members, as is usually the case when working in the assimilation paradigm. In assimilation theory, the concept of acculturation, the changing of cultural behavior of the minority in the direction of the majority society, is very important. In studying majority individuals to determine their likelihood of intermarriage with members of a minority, however, acculturation as it is usually understood is not of major importance. The majority individual in most cases need not overly concern himself or herself with a great amount of cultural change in the direction of the minority because majority attitudes and behavior are considered normative.

In assimilation theory, contact by the minority with the majority society is largely taken for granted. Contact of majority individuals with minority members, on the other hand, particularly if the minority tends to be regional in distribution, becomes problematic.

Table 13.1

Summary of Statistical Analysis of Individual Characteristics Variables

Spanish Surname Males				
Variable	Significance[1]	Strength[2]	Direction[3]	Prediction[4]
1. First Given Name	***	.18	+	P
Second Given Name	***	.27	+	P
2. Type of Ceremony	***	.31	+	P
3. Metropolitan or Non-Metropolitan Place of Birth	ns			
4. Southwest or Non-Southwest Place of Birth				
5. Generation	***	.06	+	P
6. Civilian or Military Residence	*	.06	+	P
7. Civilian or Military Identification	*	.07	+	P
8. Sex[5]	***	.07	−	P
9. Age	ns			.
10. Divorce	ns			

Table 13.1 *(continued)*

Non-Spanish Surname Males				
Variable	Significance	Strength	Direction	Prediction
1. First Given Name				
Second Given Name				
2. Type of Ceremony	***	.28	−	P
3. Metropolitan or Non-Metropolitan Place of Birth	ns			
4. Southwest or Non-Southwest Place of Birth	ns			
5. Generation				
6. Civilian or Military Residence	*	.04	+	P
7. Civilian or Military Identification	ns			
8. Sex	***	.06	+	P
9. Age	ns			
10. Divorce	ns			
Spanish Surname Females				
Variable	Significance	Strength	Direction	Prediction
1. First Given Name	*	.08	+	P
Second Given Name	ns			
2. Type of Ceremony	***	.28	+	P
3. Metropolitan or Non-Metropolitan Place of Birth	*	.06	+	P
4. Southwest or Non-Southwest Place of Birth				
5. Generation	**	.08	+	P
6. Civilian or Military Residence				
7. Civilian or Military Identification				
8. Sex	***	.07	+	P
9. Age	***	.10	+	P
10. Divorce	*	.05	+	P

(continued on page 108)

Table 13.1 (continued)

Variables	Significance	Strength	Direction	Prediction
Non-Spanish Surname Females				
1.First Given Name				
Second Given Name				
2.Type of Ceremony	***	.23	−	P
3.Metropolitan or Non-Metropolitan Place of Birth	**	.09	+	P
4.Southwest or Non-Southwest Place of Birth	**	.06	−	NP
5.Generation				
6.Civilian or Military Residence				
7.Civilian or Miliary Identification				
8.Sex	***	.06	−	P
9.Age	***	.07	−	NP
10.Divorce	*	.06	−	NP

[1]*indicates P < .05, ** P < .01, *** P < .001, ns not significant.

[2]This statistic is either Phi (for two by two contingency tables) or Cramer's V.

[3]Based on Somer's D, a +indicates a positive relationship between the variable and exogamy; a − indicates a negative relationship.

[4]P indicates directionality as predicted; NP indicates directionality not as predicted.

[5]Sex differs from the other variables in that the subgroup used to derive statistics is based not on sex and ethnicity, but only on ethnicity; that is, being either Spanish surnamed or non-Spanish surnamed. This becomes clear when one compares Table 12.1 with another table from which the above statistics are drawn, such as Table 12.3.

Going beyond the variables available in this study, we should consider other aspects of the breaking of ties theory. First of all, what factors in American life conspire to break ties? Fundamentally, ties, as I have defined them, are familial and subcommunal relationships. For minorities, their ethnicity resides to a very large extent within family and subcommunity and not in the larger society. When minority individuals interact outside of family and subcommunity, their behavior patterns change and adapt to the altered circumstances. Thus, whatever weakens family and subcommunal life in America tends to weaken ethnicity.

What, then, contributes to the breakdown of ethnic ties in the United States? Several factors clearly can be identified. One of the primary is, of course, the school, both public and parochial, in the United States. Schools take children out of the home into an English-speaking and a non-

Hispanic cultural environment. In preindustrial (particularly primitive) societies, children were not taken out of a familial environment as they progressed toward adulthood. Family members would teach the young the crafts, skills, and normative behavior suitable for that family and that subculture.

The Catholic Church, because it in general has not been an ethnic church, has performed a similar assimilating function; ethnic parishes have at best been tolerated but not encouraged[2] and are mostly to be found in very poor ethnic areas.[3] Thus, a strong correlation is created among ethnics between poverty and ethnicity.[4] The media (radio, television, and film) most certainly have a culturally assimilating effect on ethnics. Upward mobility of ethnics often involves coming in contact with more and more members of the majority on an increasingly equal basis. It also often involves geographic mobility, which tends to weaken ties to one's extended family.

The other side of the coin is that all of the above (basically institutions encouraging cultural and structural assimilation) creates a common bond between ethnics and non-ethnics and breaks down suspicion and prejudice.

What factors operate to break family ties for Anglo Americans? Interestingly, many of the same factors that break family and subcommunal ties for ethnics operate on majority individuals as well. The American school system, the church, the military, and geographic mobility all act on the majority. The egalitarianism of the American Creed (All men are created equal) works against prejudice and discrimination, which in turn work against racial and ethnic cohesion.

Although this study has not concentrated on aspects of the American economic system, we must consider its import on ethnic and familial solidarity. On the macro level, the root cause for breaking of ties is the economic system (basically monopoly capitalism) which requires a homogeneous and mobile labor force and which operates on the twin bases of universalism and achievement rather than on particularism and ascription. This weakens ethnic ties which are basically particularistic and ascriptive.

The Non-Spanish Surname Female and Breaking of Ties

Table 13.2 is a summary table of the results of our empirical analysis. As previously indicated, in 20 out of 23 cases, the relationships between the variables and exogamy are in the predicted direction. However, the three relationships not as predicted are concentrated in the non-Spanish surname female category. It could be that the reason that exogamous non-Spanish surname females tend to be younger, less likely to have been divorced, and more likely to have been born in the Southwest than their endogamous counterparts hinges upon the relative social class standing of the two groups.

A lower social class standing for exogamous non-Spanish surname females would fit neatly with the Kingsley Davis-Robert Merton proposition that females of superordinate groups who intermarry exchange their caste status for class status,[5] that is, while they marry down with reference to race or ethnicity, they marry up with reference to social class. Intermarriage in this case would be less exclusively the result of breaking of ties and contact and would also be the result of the aforementioned exchange. The relatively lower social class standing of exogamous non-Spanish surname females could explain their lower age at marriage and their lack of geographical mobility. Also, a low age of marriage is most likely related to their lower probability of having had a previous marriage.

Table 13.2
Summary of the Results of Empirical Analysis

	SSM	NSSM	SSF	NSSF
First Given Name	P		P	
Second Given Name	P			
Type of Ceremony	P	P	P	P
Metropolitan or Non-Metropolitan Place of Birth			P	P
			P	P
Southwest or Non-Southwest Place of Birth				NP
Generation	P		P	
Civilian or Military Residence	P	P		
Civilian or Military Identification	P			
Sex	P	P	P	P
Age			P	NP
Divorce			P	NP

P indicates a relationship between the variable and exogamy as predicted. NP indicates a relationship not as predicted.
Source: Table 13.1

Indeed, for Bexar County 1971, 1973, and Hidalgo County 1971, it was possible to control for previous marriage and to look at the relationship between age at marriage and exogamy for those not previously married. Table 13.3 presents the results of statistical tests for relationships between exogamy and age at marriage, controlling for previous marriage. Comparing Table 13.3 with Table 12.3 in Chapter 12, one sees that previous marriage was having an impact on the relationship between age at marriage and exogamy, particularly for non-Spanish surname females. Looking only at not previously married non-Spanish surname females, one no longer sees a significant relationship between age and exogamy.

Table 13.3

Statistical Tests for Relationships Involving Exogamy and Age[1] at Marriage by Sex and Ethnicity, Controlling for Divorce[2]

Males—Bexar County 1971, 1973, Hidalgo County 1971
Females—Bexar County 1967, 1971, 1973, Hidalgo County 1971

Sex and Ethnicity	N	Measure of Significance			Measure of Association	Measure of Directionality
		X^2	df	P	Cramer's V	Somer's D[3]
SS Male	1238	.41	2	.8129	.02	+.002
Non-SS Male	968	.46	2	.7950	.02	−.02
SS Female	1607	9.08	2	.0107	.08	+.05
Non-SS Female	1344	.89	2	.6415	.03	−.02

[1]Age categories are 1-19, 20-24, 25+.
[2]All cases are non-divorced individuals.
[3]A plus (+) Somer's D indicates an increase in the likelihood of exogamy from the first (youngest) age category, to the second category, to the third; a minus (−) indicates a decrease in the likelihood of exogamy.

Notice also that even for Spanish surname females, a control for previous marriage attenuates the relationship between age of marriage and exogamy, although the relationship remains significant at the .01 level.

Life-styles of the Intermarried

I would like to propose the following typology for the resulting life-styles in intermarriage. (See Table 13.4) I hypothesize that type 1 is the most common, followed by types 4, 3, and 2 in that order.

In general, I believe that an intermarried ethnic *ordinarily* will not emphasize his/her cultural distinctiveness wishing instead to emphasize the commonality between the spouses. Also, because of acculturation on the part of ethnic spouses, particularly third and fourth-generation Chicanos who have gone to the same schools and who have been exposed to the same media influence as members of the majority society, not much cultural distance may be left to be bridged between the ethnic and non-ethnic spouses. For these reasons, Type 1 will probably be the most common resulting life-style.

In Type 2, the non-ethnic partner learns about and tries to take on as many of the ethnic characteristics as he/she can. In the third type of intermarriage, the two go their separate ways, the ethnic involved in and participating in ethnic concerns and the non-ethnic in non-ethnic concerns. Because an emphasis on commonalities predicts greater stability in a marriage, there is the probability of less stability in this type of marriage than in the other types.

Some intermarriages have all the characteristics normally associated with solid and stable marriages. There is a mutual respect between spouses, an appreciation of both minority and majority cultural heritages, and, not uncommonly, a bilingualism (at least to some degree) on the part of the non-Hispanic. This type has been labeled a "blended" intermarriage.

Table 13.4
Intermarriage: Resulting Life-styles

Type	Description
1. Non-ethnic intermarriage	Ethnicity is not emphasized
2. All-ethnic intermarriage	The non-ethnic partner becomes very interested in and fully participates in ethnic activities
3. Dichotomous intermarriage	Each partner goes his/her own way ethnically
4. Blended intermarriage	Both try to achieve the "best of both worlds." The partners both participate in ethnic activities when they feel it appropriate and both participate in non-ethnic activities when they feel it is appropriate

Chicano Assimilation, Chicano Intermarriage, and the Future

The model of assimilation presented in Chapter 1 was derived largely from the experiences of the white ethnics, groups such as the Irish, Italians, Poles, and Jews, in the United States. There are enough differences between the situations of Mexican Americans and of other white ethnics that we cannot, as we did in Chapter 1, realistically consider complete and total absorption. Closer to reality is a model that describes considerable change on the part of the minority in the direction of the majority as well as some change of the majority in the Southwest in the direction of the minority.

Unlike the white ethnics: 1) Most Mexican Americans have physical characteristics that distinguish them as at least partially non-Caucasian. 2) Because of their historical primacy in the Southwest, there is an emphasis in the Southwest on things Mexican, such as in architecture and cuisine. Certain aspects of the ethnicity are attractive even to the majority society and, thus, to minority individuals who might not otherwise claim their heritage. 3) There are large numbers of Chicanos in the Southwest, which, in itself, slow cultural and structural assimilation. Because of significant numbers, this ethnicity becomes politically important, reaching and going beyond parity with the majority in several sub-regions of the Southwest. Because of its importance in the political arena, ethnicity is emphasized and made important to individuals. 4) The proximity of Mexico to the United States is the fourth reason. The United States shares an 1,800 mile border with Mexico, and distances from major southwestern cities to major Mexican urban areas are relatively small. The distance, for example, between San Antonio, Texas and Monterrey, Mexico (Mexico's third largest city) is only 300 miles. The distance between San Antonio and Mexico City is approximately only one-half of the distance between San Antonio and Boston. 5) Finally, the greater economic prosperity of the United States results in the continuing immigration of Mexicans, both documented and undocumented, into the United States, reinforcing the culture and adding to the numbers of the group.

In spite of the above, however, the fact of very considerable amounts of Chicano cultural, structural, and marital assimilation with the majority society is unquestionable.

When viewed over the long run, as in Table 6.1 in Chapter 6, the rates of Chicano-Anglo intermarriage have been slowly increasing. It is not inconceivable, however, that the movement of the Mexican American people culturally, socially, and maritally toward the majority society may stop and even reverse itself.[6] For example, events such as a war with Mexico, a communist government in Mexico, or a severe depression in the United States, could seriously affect Chicano-Anglo relations and lead to decreasing rates of intermarriage.

Ultimately the increase or decrease of Chicano intermarriage will depend in large measure on the attitudes and behavior of the Anglo majority toward Chicanos. General acceptance of Chicanos by Anglos and significant and continuous Chicano upward mobility, it seems to me, will lead to increasing rates of intermarriage. A rise in the amount of prejudice and discrimination directed toward Chicanos and their relegation to barrios and to the lower social classes will result in the polarization of the two groups and in decreasing rates of intermarriage.

In the case of increased acceptance of the minority by the majority, however, clearly a desired state of affairs and at this time the most likely, there lies a problem which must be faced by Chicanos. Increased acceptance by the majority and upward social mobility of Chicanos lead to cultural and structural assimilation and to intermarriage. This results in a loss of ethnic cohesion and in a loss of the ethnic language and culture, not a desirable state of affairs for many Chicanos. Cultural maintenance in an open society will be one of the major issues to be faced by Chicanos in the future.[7]

Notes

1. Contact is the positive side of breaking of ties theory. Not only must one break away *from*, but one must come into contact *with*, and these two processes occur simultaneously.
2. The other side of it, of course, is that the church can be credited with attempting to mainstream and integrate its many poor into the larger American society.
3. Even here, because of the shortage of Mexican American priests, one still observes the phenomenon of a congregation almost entirely composed of Mexican Americans following the lead of the one non-Hispanic, the priest, in the church. Contrast this with the many black ministers of churches.
4. This correlation is created not only by the church but by many other social institutions, and one senses that to move out of poverty, ethnicity must be shed.
5. Kingsley Davis, "Intermarriage in Caste Societies," *American Anthropologist*, 43 (1941), pp. 376-395. Robert K. Merton, "Intermarriage and the Social Structure: Fact and Theory," *Psychiatry*, 4 (August 1941), pp. 361-374.
6. Already the political and cultural consciousness generated by the Chicano Movement has had an impact on the cultural and structural assimilation of some Chicano subgroups, notably those involved in academia. The impact has been to slow and, in some cases, even to reverse cultural and structural assimilation.
7. Bilingual-bicultural schools aimed not at "Americanizing" Chicanos but rather at cultural maintenance are a sign that this issue is coming to the forefront.

APPENDICES

A: Codebook, County Marriage Data

Variable	Description	Col.	Range	Missing
ID	Case Number	1-5		
FORM	Number of Marriage Application Form	6-11		
CO	County	12	1-4	
YEAR	Year of Marriage	13-14		
MARTYP	Type of Marriage, Endogamous or Exogamous	15	1-4	9
CERTYP	Type of Ceremony	16	1-6	9
MSNAM	Ethnicity of Male's Surname	17	1-3	9
M1GN	Ethnicity of Male's First Given Name	18	1-3	9
M2GN	Ethnicity of Male's Second Given Name	19	1-3	9
RESM	Male's Residence at Marriage, Civilian or Military	20	1-2	9
AGEM	Male's Age at Last Birthday	21-22		99
BPM	Male's Birthplace	23-24	1-10	99
MNMM	Male's Place of Birth, Metropolitan or Non-Metropolitan	25	1-2	9
*RACEM	Male's Race	26	1-5	9
IDM	Male's Source of ID	27	1-2	9
DIVM	Male's Previous Divorce	28	1-2	9
*DIVRM	Male's Divorce Within Six Months	29	1-2	9
FSNAM	Ethnicity of Female's Surname	30	1-3	9
F1GN	Ethnicity of Female's First Given Name	31	1-3	9
F2GN	Ethnicity of Female's Second Given Name	32	1-3	9
RESF	Female's Residence at Marriage, Civilian or Military	33	1-2	9
AGEF	Female's Age at Last Birthday	34-35		99
BPF	Female's Birthplace	36-37	1-10	99
MNMF	Female's Place of Birth, Metropolitan or Non-Metropolitan	38	1-2	9
*RACEF	Female's Race	39	1-5	9
IDF	Female's Source of ID	40	1-2	9
DIVF	Female's Previous Divorce	41	1-2	9
*DIVRF	Female's Divorce Within Six Months	42	1-2	9
*MONTH	Month of Marriage	43-44	1-12	99

*This variable is not developed in this study.

B: *Variable Scores, County Marriage Data*

Column	Variable	Variable Value
1-5	ID	Case Number
6-11	Form Number	Number on Marriage Application Form
12	County	Bexar = 1
		Nueces = 2
		Hidalgo = 3
		Bernalillo = 4
13-14	Year of Marriage	
15	Type of Marriage	Non-SS Male and Non-SS Female = 1
		Non-SS Male and SS Female = 2
		SS Male and Non-SS Female = 3
		SS Male and SS Female = 4
16	Type of Ceremony	Catholic = 1
		Jewish = 2
		Protestant Church = 3
		Protestant Sect = 4
		Other = 5
		Civil = 6
		Military = 7
17	Ethnicity of Male's Surname	Clearly SS = 1
		Clearly Non-SS = 2
		Undetermined = 3
18	Ethnicity of Male's First Given Name	Clearly SS = 1
		Clearly Non-SS = 2
		Undetermined = 3
19	Ethnicity of Male's Second Given Name	Clearly SS = 1
		Clearly Non-SS = 2
		Undetermined = 3
20	Male's Residence at Marriage	Civilian = 1
		Military = 2
21-22	Male's Age at Marriage	

Column	Variable	Variable Value
23-24	Male's Birthplace	Local =01
		Texas =02
		New Mexico =03
		California =04
		Arizona =05
		Colorado =06
		The South =07
		Non-South =08
		Mexico = 10
		Other Foreign = 11
		Puerto Rico = 12
25	Male's Origin	Metropolitan =1
		Non-Metropolitan =2
26	Male's Race	White =1
		Black =2
		Oriental =3
		Other =4
		Native American =5
27	Male's Source of ID	Civilian =1
		Military =2
28	Male's Previous Marital Status	Not Divorced =1
		Divorced =2
29	Male's Divorce Within Six Months of Marriage	Over 6 Months =1
		6 Months or Less =2
30	Ethnicity of Female's Surname	Clearly SS =1
		Clearly Non-SS =2
		Undetermined =3
31	Ethnicity of Female's First Given Name	Clearly SS =1
		Clearly Non-SS =2
		Undetermined =3
32	Ethnicity of Female's Second Given Name	Clearly SS =1
		Clearly Non-SS =2
		Undetermined =3

B: *Variable Scores, County Marriage Data (continued)*

Column	Variable	Variable Value
33	Female's Residence at Marriage	Civilian = 1 Military = 2
34-35	Female's Age At Marriage	
36-37	Female's Birthplace	Local = 01 Texas = 02 New Mexico = 03 California = 04 Arizona = 05 Colorado = 06 The South = 07 Non-South = 08 Mexico = 10 Other Foreign = 11 Puerto Rico = 12
38	Female's Origin	Metropolitan = 1 Non-Metropolitan = 2
39	Female's Race	White = 1 Black = 2 Oriental = 3 Other = 4 Native American = 5
40	Female's Source of ID	Civilian = 1 Military = 2
41	Female's Previous Marital Status	Not Divorced = 1 Divorced = 2
42	Female's Divorce Within Six Months of Marriage	Over 6 Months = 1 6 Months or Less = 2

C: Variables Available By County and Year[1]

County	Bexar				Bernalillo		Nueces				Hidalgo	
Year	1964	1967	1971	1973	1967	1971	1960[2]	1961[2]	1970[2]	1971[2]	1961[2]	1971
Variable												
ID	*	*	*	*	*	*	*	*	*	*	*	*
FORM	*	*	*	*	*	*	*	*	*	*	*	*
CO	*	*	*	*	*	*	*	*	*	*	*	*
YEAR	*	*	*	*	*	*	*	*	*	*	*	*
MARTYP	*	*	*	*	*	*	*	*	*	*	*	*
CERTYP	-	-	-	-	*	*	-	-	-	-	-	-
MSNAM	*	*	*	*	*	*	*	*	*	*	*	*
M1GN	*	*	*	-	-	-	*	*	*	*	-	-
M2GN	*	*	*	-	-	-	*	*	*	*	-	-
RESM	*	*	*	*	*	-	-	-	-	-	-	-
AGEM	*	*	*	*	*	*	-	-	-	-	*	*
BPM	-	*	*	*	*	*	-	-	-	-	*	*
MNMM	-	*	*	*	*	*	-	-	-	-	*	*
RACEM[3]	-	*	*	*	-	-	*	*	*	*	-	-
IDM	-	*	*	*	-	-	-	-	-	-	-	-
DIVM	-	-	*	*	-	-	-	-	-	-	-	*
DIVRM[3]	-	-	*	*	-	-	-	-	-	-	-	-
FSNAM	*	*	*	*	*	*	*	*	*	*	*	*
F1GN	*	*	*	-	-	-	*	*	*	*	*	-
F2GN	*	*	*	-	-	-	*	*	*	*	*	-
RESF	*	*	*	*	*	-	-	-	-	-	-	-
AGEF	*	*	*	*	*	*	-	-	-	-	*	*
BPF	-	*	*	*	*	*	-	-	-	-	*	*
MNMF	-	*	*	*	*	*	-	-	-	-	*	*
RACEF[3]	-	*	*	*	-	-	*	*	*	*	-	-
IDF	-	*	*	*	-	-	-	-	-	-	-	-
DIVF	-	*	*	*	-	-	-	-	-	-	-	*
DIVRF[3]	-	-	*	*	-	-	-	-	-	-	-	-
MONTH	*	*	*	*	*	*	*	*	*	*	*	*

[1] An asterisk (*) indicates that a variable is available for the indicated county and year; a dash (-) indicates that the varible is not available.

[2] Data for these counties and years includes only exogamous individuals; hence they were excluded from crosstabulation analysis.

[3] This variable is not analyzed in this study.

D: Standard Metropolitan Statistical Areas, 1970

Texas

Abilene
Amarillo
Austin
Beaumont—Port Arthur—Orange
Brownsville—Harlingen—San Benito
Bryan—College Station
Corpus Christi
Dallas
El Paso
Fort Worth
Galveston—Texas City
Houston
Laredo
Lubbock
McAllen—Pharr—Edinburg
Midland
Odessa
San Angelo
San Antonio
Sherman-Denison
Texarkana
Tyler
Waco
Wichita Falls

New Mexico

Albuquerque

E: Codebook II

Variable	Description	Col.	Range	Missing
ID	Case Number	1-5		
SEX	Sex	6	1-2	
FORM	Number on Marriage Application Form	7-12		
CO	County	13	1-4	
YEAR	Year of Marriage	14-15		
MARTYP	Type of Marriage, Endogamous or Exogamous	16	1-4	9
CERTYP	Type of Ceremony	17	1-6	9
SNAM	Ethnicity of Surname	18	1-3	9
GNM1	Ethnicity of First Given Name	19	1-3	9
GNM2	Ethnicity of Second Given Name	20	1-3	9
RES	Residence at Marriage, Civilian or Military	21	1-2	9
AGE	Age at Last Birthday	22-23		99
BP	Birthplace	24-25	1-10	99
MNM	Origin, Metro or Non-Metro	26	1-2	9
RACE	Race	27	1-5	9
IDS	Source of ID	28	1-2	9
DIV	Previous Divorce	29	1-2	9
DIVR	Divorce Within Six Months	30	1-2	9
MONTH	Month of Marriage	31-32	1-12	99

Bibliography

Alvírez, David and Bean, Frank D. "The Mexican American Family," in *Ethnic Families in America*. Ed. C. H. Mindel and R. W. Habenstein. New York: Elsevier, 1976.

Bean, Frank D. and Bradshaw, Benjamin S. "Intermarriage Between Persons of Spanish and Non-Spanish Surname: Changes from Mid-Nineteenth to the Mid-Twentieth Century," *Social Science Quarterly*, 51 (September 1970), pp. 389-395.

Blalock, Hubert M., Jr. *Social Statistics*. New York: McGraw-Hill, 1972.

_____. *Theory Construction*. Englewood Cliffs: Prentice-Hall, 1969.

Bogardus, Emory S. "Comparing Racial Distance in Ethiopia, South Africa, and the United States," *Sociology and Social Research*, 52 (January, 1968), p. 152.

Bradshaw, Benjamin S. "Some Demographic Aspects of Marriage: A Comparative Study of Three Ethnic Groups." Master's Thesis, University of Texas at Austin, 1960.

Briggs, Vernon M., Fogel, Walter and Schmidt, Fred H. *The Chicano Worker*. Austin: The University of Texas Press, 1977.

Bugelski, B. R. "Assimilation Through Intermarriage," *Social Forces*, 40 (December, 1961), pp. 148-153.

Burgess, Ernest W. and Wallin, Paul. "Homogamy in Social Characteristics," *American Journal of Sociology*, 49 (September, 1943), pp. 109-124.

Burma, John H. "Interethnic Marriage in Los Angeles, 1948-1959," *Social Forces*, 42 (1963), pp. 156-165.

Burma, John H., Cretser, Gary A. and Leon, Joseph J. "Confidential and Non-Confidential Marriage: A Study of Spanish Surnamed Marriages in San Bernardino County, California, 1970-1977," *Marriage and Family Counselors Quarterly*, 13 (1979), p. 2.

Centers, Richard. "Marital Selection and Occupational Strata," *American Journal of Sociology*, 54 (1949), pp. 530-35.

Coronado, Jim. "Ladies, Allay Men's Fears: Ask a Guy to Lunch Today," *The Daily Texan*, May 5, 1977.

Davis, Kingsley. "Intermarriage in Caste Societies," *American Anthropologist*, 43 (1941), pp. 376-395.

Druss, R. "Foreign Marriages in the Military," *Psychiatrics Quarterly* (1965), pp. 220-226.

Fitzpatrick, Joseph P. "Intermarriage of Puerto Ricans in New York City," *American Journal of Sociology*, 71 (January, 1966), pp. 396-406.

Gans, Herbert J. *The Urban Villagers.* New York: The Free Press, 1965.

Gardner, Richard. *Grito! Reis Tijerina and the New Mexico Land Grant War of 1967.* New York: Harper and Row, 1971.

Glick, Paul C. *American Families.* New York: John Wiley and Sons, Inc., 1958.

_____. "Intermarriage and Fertility Patterns Among Persons in Major Religious Groups," *Eugenics Quarterly,* 7 (1960), pp. 31-8.

Golden, Joseph, cited by Albert I. Gordon in *Intermarriage.* Boston: Beacon Press, 1964, p. 60.

González, Nancie L. *The Spanish-Americans of New Mexico: A Heritage of Pride.* Albuquerque: The University of New Mexico Press, 1969.

Gordon, Albert I. *Intermarriage.* Boston: Beacon Press, 1964.

Gordon, Milton M. *Assimilation in American Life.* New York: Oxford University Press, 1964.

Grebler, Leo, Moore, Joan W. and Guzman, Ralph C. *The Mexican-American People: The Nation's Second Largest Minority.* New York: The Free Press, 1970.

Greeley, Andrew M. *Ethnicity in the United States.* New York: John Wiley and Sons, 1974.

Gutiérrez, José Angel. "22 Miles," in *Aztlan: An Anthology of Mexican American Literature.* Ed. by Luis Valdez and Stan Steiner. New York: Vintage Books, 1972, p. 330.

Heer, David. "Negro-White Marriage in the United States," *Journal of Marriage and the Family* 28 (August, 1966), pp. 262-73.

_____. "The Prevalence of Black-White Marriage in the United States, 1960 and 1970," *Journal of Marriage and the Family* (May, 1974), pp. 246-58.

Herberg, Will. *Protestant-Catholic-Jew.* Garden City, New York: Doubleday, 1956.

Hernandez, José, Estrada, Leobardo L. and Alvírez, David. "Census Data and the Problem of Conceptually Defining the Mexican American Population," *Social Science Quarterly,* 53 (March, 1973), pp. 671-87.

Hollingshead, August B. "Cultural Factors in the Selection of Marriage Mates," *American Sociological Review,* 15 (1950), pp. 619-627.

• Holscher, Louis, Varni, Charles and Naranjo, Letty. "Chicano Exogamous Marriages in New Mexico." Paper Presented at the Annual Meeting of the Pacific Sociological Association, Anaheim, California (1979).

Kennedy, Ruby Jo Reeves. "Single or Triple Melting-Pot? Intermarriage Trends in New Haven, 1870-1940," *American Journal of Sociology,* 49 (January, 1944), pp. 331-39.

_____. "Single or Triple Melting-Pot? Intermarriage in New Haven, 1870-1950," *American Journal of Sociology,* 58 (July, 1952), pp. 56-59.

Kikumura, A. and Kitano, H. L. L. "Interracial Marriage: A Picture of the Japanese-Americans," *Journal of Social Issues*, 29 (1973), pp. 67-81.

Little, Roger W. "The Military Family," in *Handbook of Military Institutions*. Ed. by Roger W. Little. Beverly Hills Sage Publications, 1971.

Madsen, William *The Mexican-Americans of South Texas*. San Francisco: Holt, Rinehart and Winston, 1964.

Matthiessen, Peter. *Sal Si Puedes: Cesar Chavez and the New American Revolution*. New York: Dell Publishing Company, 1973.

McWilliams, Carey. *North From Mexico*. New York: Greenwood Press, 1968.

Merton, Robert K. "Intermarriage and the Social Structure: Fact and Theory," *Psychiatry* 4 (August, 1941), pp. 361-74.

Mittelbach, Frank G. and Moore, Joan W. "Ethnic Endogamy – The Case of Mexican Americans," *American Journal of Sociology*, 74 (1968), pp. 50-62.

Mittelbach, Frank G., Moore, Joan W. and McDaniel, Ronald. *Intermarriage of Mexican-Americans, Advance Report 6*. Los Angeles: Graduate School of Business Administration, The University of California, 1966.

Murguía, Edward. *Assimilation, Colonialism and the Mexican American People*. Austin: Center for Mexican American Studies, The University of Texas at Austin, 1975.

Murguía, Edward and Frisbie, W. Parker. "Trends in Mexican American Intermarriage: Recent Finding in Perspective," *Social Science Quarterly*, 53 (December, 1977), pp. 374-389.

Moskos, Charles C., Jr. "Minority Groups in Military Organization," in *Handbook of Military Institutions*. Ed. by Roger W. Little. Beverly Hills, Sage Publications, 1971.

Myrdal, Gunnar. *An American Dilemma*. New York: Harper and Brothers, 1944.

Nie, Norman H. et al. *Statistical Package for the Social Sciences*. New York: McGraw-Hill, 1975.

Panunzio, Constantine. "Intermarriage in Los Angeles, 1924-33," *American Journal of Sociology*, 47 (1942), pp. 690-701.

Park, Robert E. *Race and Culture*. Glencoe: The Free Press, 1959.

_____. "Social Assimilation" in *Encyclopedia of the Social Sciences*. Ed. by Alvin Johnson. New York: Macmillan, 1935.

Park, Robert E. and Burgess, Ernest. *Introduction to the Science of Sociology*. Chicago: The University of Chicago Press, 1924.

Rendon, Armando B. *Chicano Manifesto*. New York: Macmillan, 1971.

Reuter, E. B. Quoted by Brewton Berry in *Race and Ethnic Relations*. 3d ed. Boston: Houghton Mifflin Company, 1963, pp. 273-74.

Rodman, Hyman. "Technical Note on Two Rates of Mixed Marriage," *American Sociological Review*, 30 (1965), pp. 776-78.

Rubel, Arthur J. *Across the Tracks: Mexican-Americans in a Texas City*. Austin: The University of Texas Press, 1966.

Scott, John F. "The Role of the College Sorority in Endogamy," *American Sociological Review*, 30 (August, 1965), pp. 514-527.

Sherif, Muzafer. "Experiments in Group Conflict," *Scientific American* 195 (1956), pp. 54-58.

Sherif, Muzafer, et al. *Intergroup Conflict and Cooperation: The Robbers Cave Experiment*. Norman, Oklahoma: The University of Oklahoma Book Exchange, 1961.

Shockley, John Staples. *Chicano Revolt in a Texas Town*. Notre Dame: The University of Notre Dame Press, 1974.

Schoen, Robert, Nelson, Verne E. and Collins, Marion. "Intermarriage Among Spanish Surnamed Californians, 1962-1974," *International Migration Review*, 12 (1978), pp. 359-369.

Simons, Sarah E. "Social Assimilation," *American Journal of Sociology*, 6 (1901), pp. 790-822.

Smith, William C. *Americans in the Making*. New York: D. Appleton-Century Company, Inc., 1939.

Stone, Robert C., Petroni, Frank A. and McCleneghan, Thomas J. "Nogales, Arizona: An Overview of Economic and Interethnic Patterns in a Border Community," *Arizona Review of Business and Public Research*, 12 (January, 1963), pp. 4-29.

Strauss, Anselm, cited by Richard Udry in *The Social Context of Marriage*. Philadelphia: J. B. Lippencott Company, 1966, p. 205.

Thomas, John L. "The Factor of Religion in the Selection of Marriage Mates," *American Sociological Review*, 16 (August, 1951), pp. 487-91.

"Thumbs Up/Thumbs Down," *Nuestro*, 2 (April, 1978) p. 80.

"Thumbs Up/Thumbs Down," *Nuestro*, 2 (August, 1978) p. 50.

Udry, J. Richard. *The Social Context of Marriage*. Philadelphia: J. B. Lippencott Company, 1966.

United States Department of Commerce, Social and Economic Statistics Administration, Bureau of the Census, 1970 Census of Population, PC(S1)-60, Table 1.

_____, PC(S1)-61, Table 1.

_____, PC(1)-C33, Table 43.

_____, PC(1)-C45, Table 43.

United States Department of Health, Education and Welfare, A Study of Selected Socio-Economic Characteristics of Ethnic Minorities, Based on the 1970 Census, Volume I: Americans of Spanish Origin. Washington, D.C.: U.S. Government Printing Office, 1974.

Vander Zanden, James W. *American Minority Relations* 2d ed. New York: The Ronald Press Company, 1966.

Warner, W. Lloyd and Associates. *Democracy in Jonesville.* New York: Harper and Brother, 1949.

Warner, W. Lloyd and Srole, Leo. *The Social Systems of American Ethnic Groups.* New Haven: Yale University Press, 1945.

Wessel, B. B., cited by Brewton Berry in *Race and Ethnic Relations.* 3d ed. Boston: Houghton Mifflin Company, 1965, pp. 289-90.

Name Index

Subject Index

DATE DUE

APR 0 4 1996		
MAR 1 9 1996		
MAY 1 3 1998		
JUN 1 2 1998		
JUN 1 3 1998		
NOV 1 3 2000		
NOV 0 1 2007		
MAR 1 1 2008		
RENEWALS 362-8433